DUBAI

AN INSIDER'S
GUIDE

—

SUJIT SHOME

Published by Sujit Shome

ISBN: 978-1-9164678-0-4

Cover design, illustration & interior formatting:
Mark Thomas / Coverness.com (via Reedsy.com)

TABLE OF CONTENTS

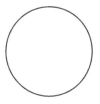

INTRODUCTION

Dubai. DXB. Do-Buy. The Las Vegas of the East, minus the casinos. South Asia's very own Panama City in the desert. Call it whatever you want, but just about everyone in the world knows about this city. It's easy to reach, too: just hop on an Emirates Airlines flight from London, New York, Mumbai, Melbourne, Toronto, Tokyo, Rio, Cairo, or Bangkok—in fact, from almost any city, anywhere in the world—and you'll soon be in the wonderland known as Dubai.

Of course, in going there, there is also the small matter of your wallet. Don't leave your debit and credit cards at home, because when you are in Dubai, you are expected to shop "'til you drop," as the saying goes. You will shop at the Emirates Mall. You will shop in the Gold Souk. On your way back home, before you are safely ensconced in the comforts of your Emirates flight and in the care of its super-efficient cabin staff, you will have shopped at the world-famous Dubai Duty-Free Store in the airport.

This book is dedicated to all the fantastic foreigners who come from all over the world to make Dubai their temporary home. These are the people who actually built Dubai. The three words used to describe these people—expats, immigrants, and foreigners—are used interchangeably in this book, though strictly speaking, they are not exactly interchangeable in Dubai.

In Dubai, "expats" are the "posh" foreigners. They are the highly qualified professionals or successful businessmen who enjoy a very high quality of life. Generally speaking, they employ their own household help, live in luxurious villas, and may also have chauffeurs to drive them around. In essence, they enjoy the kind of lifestyle that most people dream of even in the West.

But "expats" aren't the only foreigners who live and work in Dubai. Migrant workers from Asia and Africa come to Dubai in droves with dreams of securing a better life for themselves and their families. In Dubai, they lead marginal lives as labourers that are only slightly better than what they experienced back home.

It is important to keep in mind that, strictly speaking, there is no such thing as "immigration" in Dubai. Elsewhere in the world, immigrants are foreigners who move to a new country, put down roots there, and settle down permanently. In Dubai, once a foreigner's visa expires, their time is up, and they must leave. There is no such thing as permanent residency or gaining citizenship.

This book is also intended for the new group of professionals and business owners from all over the world who are planning to make Dubai their home and run their businesses from there. They are all charged up and raring to go for Dubai's 2020 EXPO. This event is the prime catalyst for a potential stampede of several million "Dubai Dreamers." These individuals need to know Dubai's real story before they decide to move there, and I have endeavoured to tell it here.

The information presented in this book is based on my thirty-plus years of close association with Dubai, including ten years of residence there. During that time, I was lucky enough to interact with every single section of Dubai society, including a wide range of locals—the term for UAE nationals—which is very rare for foreigners. This not only gave me a great deal of insight into how the commercial aspects of Dubai operate, but it also gave me an unparalleled look into the local society's attitude towards the foreigners who constitute 90 percent of Dubai's population. Painstaking research and countless interviews also helped me bring to light many events with which I was not personally involved.

This is Dubai's real story, and I must warn you that this is not a politically correct book. Everything here is based on my personal experiences, opinions, knowledge, research, interviews, and memories. I do not claim that these are the experiences or views of anyone other than my interviewees and myself. I also disclaim any liability, loss, or risk incurred by individuals or groups who act on the information contained herein. Every single legal entity, whether individuals or businesses, have different circumstances, and they must consult their own accredited professional advisers before taking any action in regards to any matter discussed in this book.

Please note that "Dhs" refers to Dubai's currency, the Dirham; "Rs" refers to Indian Rupees; and "USD," of course, refers to the mighty U.S. greenback. "Fils" is the equivalent of cents, the lesser currency in Dubai. The Dirham, like the currency of all Gulf nations, is tied to the U.S. dollar, and as of July 2018, one U.S. dollar is equivalent to 3.67 Dirhams.

Also, for my readers from different parts of the world, the words "cheque" and "check" refer to the same good old-fashioned banking instrument. Names have been changed to protect the individuals' identities.

Finally, please note that this book provides quite a few examples of people from the Indian subcontinent due to the large number of guest workers from that region. As you will see throughout the course of this book, individuals from different nations and of different ethnicities can have vastly different experiences in Dubai.

So, with all that said, let's get cracking!

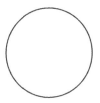

MUST-KNOW ARABIC IN DUBAI

Although Dubai is in the Arabian Peninsula and is the second-largest city in the United Arab Emirates (UAE) after Abu Dhabi, one does not actually need to speak any Arabic to get by in Dubai. In fact, there are many non-Arab foreigners who have lived in Dubai for many decades and cannot even string together a single sentence in Arabic. Nearly everyone speaks English, and all expats speak their own native tongues, such as Hindi, Urdu, Tagalog, Malayalam, Sinhalese, English, Bengali, Farsi, etc., in their own communities. However, the following words or phrases fall into the category of "must-know" Arabic for a comfortable experience in Dubai:

1. ***Salam ale Khoum***: Greetings. You should also know its counter greeting, *Ale Khoum Salam.*
2. ***Fulus***: Money/Cash. This is the most important word in Dubai. Nothing else matters more in Dubai, as we will see.

3. ***Wasta***: Influence/Connections. This is possibly as powerful a word as *fulus*. I have devoted an entire section to this great word.

4. ***Surta:*** Police. A very important word in a totalitarian police state, which is precisely what Dubai is.

5. ***Khabri:*** Plain-clothes police. Like the regular police, they are very important in Dubai's society. They can stop expats anytime, anywhere, and for any reason, so never leave your residence without your personal ID papers in the form of your Labour Card, or *pataka*, as it is called.

6. ***Habibi:*** A term of endearment for men, and ***Habibthi***: A term of endearment for women. Men, especially foreign men, are strictly advised not to get too familiar with local women and use this term casually, even if they are used to doing so in their home countries. If they call a local woman *habibthi*, they are asking for serious trouble. This is especially relevant for those who casually use the words "love" or "darling" in the West or "*pyare*" in the East.

7. ***Arbab***: Boss, sir, seth, malik, the owner of a business, etc. This is mostly used to show grovelling respect to local men.

8. ***Maafi Mushkil***: No (*maafi*) problem (*mushkil*). Everyone uses this word constantly, every day, everywhere, all day, all year long. In Dubai, everything is "no problem."

9. ***Khalas***: Finished, over, end of. Any discussions that can be become complicated, such as conversations about money or visas, are finished with "*khalas*."

10. ***Khalli Walli***: Get lost! This is the Dubai equivalent of "f— off" in English, just without the sexual innuendo. This is an extremely popular word in Dubai and is used almost as much as *fulus* and *wasta*. All foreigners pick it up quickly.

11. ***Masalam:*** Goodbye.

12. ***Sukran:*** Thank you.

13. ***Aiwaa***: Yes. In reality, it's more of a "Yeeess! Yeah! Done!" It's just shy of a really enthusiastic high-five. This is because everything is always "Yes" in ever-positive Dubai.

14. ***Kandura***: The white, gown-like tunic worn by most local men in Dubai. It is the principal local dress. Not all men who wear it are sheikhs—the title of the local ruling elite—though that is a common misperception among foreigners and new arrivals in Dubai. It is the power apparel, which distinguishes a local from a foreigner.

So there you go: the fourteen Arabic words or phrases you need to get by in Dubai, whether you're there for a short, seven-day vacation or a stay of several decades.

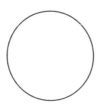

DUBAI'S ROYAL FAMILY AND GOVERNMENT STRUCTURE: A GENERAL OVERVIEW

As a country, the United Arab Emirates (UAE) is a federation of seven emirates/regions, which are ruled by emirs/sheikhs. These seven regions are Abu Dhabi, Dubai, Sharjah, Ajman, Ras al Khaimah, Fujeraih, and Umm al Quwain. Abu Dhabi is the capital and has most of the country's oil wealth, while Dubai is the nation's commercial and tourist hub. It has very little oil wealth compared to Abu Dhabi. These two emirates have most of the nation's *fulus*, or money, and *wasta*, or influence.

Accordingly, Dubai's ruling family, the Al Maktoums, hold the country's prime ministerial position, while Abu Dhabi's ruling family, the Al Nahyans, are accorded the country's highest political position, the presidency. The rest of the emirates have little money from either oil or trade and commerce, so they have little say in how the country is run. Most of these other emirates are reportedly dependent on support from Abu Dhabi.

Without oil reserves to depend upon, most of these other regions are forming or have formed what are known as "Free Zones" and industrial areas to attract foreign investments. Given Dubai's horrendous and ever-increasing cost of living, these areas, especially Ajman, Fujairah, and Ras al-Khaimah, should be actively considered as potential business destinations as an alternative to Dubai, though after thorough research and investigation.

The Al Maktoum family rules Dubai like autocratic monarchs. They are considered either benevolent dictators or crude autocrats, depending on one's attitude toward and personal experience with Dubai's government. Through their administrative machinery, the royal family tightly controls all information that comes into and goes out of the country. For years, censorship of books, magazines, newspapers, television, and movies have been common. In the wake of the Arab Spring, which was heavily fuelled by social media, most Middle Eastern rulers, including the Al Maktoums, also began to monitor social media use and block certain websites in order to further control the flow of information. As a result, most knowledge and information about the rulers of Middle Eastern countries and cities, such as Dubai, is based on rumours and hearsay.

As a result, no one in the expat community actually knows where the Al Maktoums are from. Many stories about the family and how they came to rule Dubai circulate, but nothing can be officially verified. Some claim they are Arabs with a long history in the area, while others claim they are actually Iranian in origin. Even Google searches are not helpful or reliable in this. No one actually knows or even cares about such trivialities in Dubai.

The current ruler of Dubai, Sheikh Mohamed Bin Rashid Al Maktoum—which means Mohamed, the son of Rashid, of the Al Maktoum family—is the youngest of the late Sheikh Rashid's three sons. Sheikh Rashid was the founder of modern Dubai, the man that initiated its transformation from a sleepy fishing village into a modern bustling metropolis. He laid the basic foundations of its free trade economy and lack of personal taxes, despite its lack of oil reserves. Following in his father's footsteps, Sheikh Mohamed is the modern face of modern Dubai: he uses social media such as LinkedIn and Facebook and has been credited with transforming Dubai into the global, cosmopolitan city it is today. But despite his modern approach and practices, Sheikh Mohamed continues to run Dubai with an iron fist, just as his father did and as his son, the Crown Prince of Dubai, Sheikh Hamdan Bin Mohammed Bin Rashid Al Maktoum, will after him.

There are a great many stories and rumours about Dubai's "leadership team," as the emirate's rulers like to call themselves today, making use of corporate buzzwords. Each story is spicier than the last, and they are handed down from one generation of expats to another.

There are countless exciting stories about Sheikh Mohamed

himself: "I saw him driving an old, battered Mercedes, and he was patiently waiting next to me at a traffic light," or "I heard that he often follows the Dubai municipality trucks to make sure they're cleaning the roads properly."

In Dubai, the number on a car's licence plate denotes the owner's power and wealth. The lower the number, the more significant the power. As a result, Sheikh Mohamed's car is likely registered with the Dubai number plate "1." It is highly unlikely that a car with such a registration number would be following a Dubai municipality truck around to see if its expat driver was picking up the garbage bins properly. Besides, he has more than enough people to do such things for him.

However, these stories are very much in the spirit of those told about Sheikh Rashid, Sheikh Mohamed's father. According to this folklore, Sheikh Rashid personally supervised every single major project that Dubai initiated in the 1960s, '70s, and early '80s. The story also goes that, every day, he would personally sit at the toll points on the newly built Al Maktoum bridge connecting Pur Dubai to Deira and collect the bridge toll as the cars crossed the Dubai Creek.

It's said that Sheikh Rashid was an extremely tolerant ruler who embraced every single community and religion within his territory. When he died in 1990 after not having been seen in public for many years, the Asian shopkeepers in Pur Dubai voluntarily closed their shops for two whole days as a mark of respect for the late ruler.

Still, however much the late Sheikh Rashid may have appreciated the contributions of Dubai's large foreign community, not one single documented foreigner from any non-Gulf state can boast of possessing a UAE passport. Some have spent forty or fifty years—if not more—in the desert, supporting and driving Dubai's economy forward through their enterprise and hard work, but none have gained UAE citizenship and a passport for their brilliant efforts and contributions.

Dubai and the rest of the Gulf states treat foreigners with the mindset that even if they are worth millions, foreigners are their slaves while they are there. They expect foreigners to come to the desert, work hard, make millions for them, spend every penny they earn there, and then just go back home afterwards with nothing to show for it.

But immigrants in general are a very determined and entrepreneurial lot, and they never give up. According to a senior expat working in a government bank in Dubai, a group of expats living and working in Dubai have reportedly approached the United Nations for help, pointing out that they have invested everything in this desert land: their energy, money, time, and even their dignity. All they want in return is to be able to call the UAE their home. Of course, these expats have kept their petition extremely hush-hush, because they are afraid of the very real possibility of severe repercussions from both the government and their employers.

Allegedly, this is not the first time expats have asked for the right to formally immigrate to the country, but the UAE's government has consistently resisted such requests. The government argues that because they are a very small country, they need to tightly control their population numbers. Hence, they cannot allow a flood of foreigners to become permanent residents, regardless of how many years they have lived in and contributed to the country.

Of course, the UAE does not mind hard-working, highly skilled foreigners; otherwise, who would do the actual work of keeping the economy going and training the next generation of locals? In particular, they love wealthy foreign investors; super-rich socialites; deposed dictators; foreign politicians; and anyone else with a combination of wealth and influence. Show them your money, and magically, the gates of Dubai will be flung open for you at breakneck speed.

In essence, Dubai wants foreigners' money; their education; their global experience, knowledge, and connections; and their skills. Nothing more. Of course, to be fair to Dubai, all countries in the world want this, but Dubai's approach is uniquely short-term. After the local economy has taken advantage of everything a foreigner has to offer, it wants them gone. There is never a lifelong invitation to stay and "put down roots," and as a result, it is very much an "Us versus Them" society. Still, there are a great many expats who have lived in Dubai for decades and shudder at the thought of having to leave and go back to where they came from.

Of course, Dubai is conscious of its international appeal and does not want to actively scare away potential foreign investors. Sheikh Mohamed is the main driver and brand ambassador of modern Dubai, and his media team, which works relentlessly in the Western media, portrays him as a "cool," hip, modern sheikh. For the most part, they are effective. For example, they recently made use of his taking the London Underground while on a visit to that city, spinning it as an example of how cool, hip, and relatable he is. His son, Sheikh Hamdan, also uses his LinkedIn account to post links to videos of his father twerking, further playing up the cool, hip hop image of Dubai's current ruler.

Sheikh Mohamed also has a talent for dramatic, attention-stealing projects. He built the world's tallest building, Burj Khalifa, standing 828 meters (2716.5 feet) tall, as well as a full-size indoor ice-skating rink in a country where outside temperatures are regularly over 50 degrees centigrade (122 degrees Fahrenheit) for most of the year. He has plans to build a replica of the Taj Mahal and is holding a huge Business Expo in 2020 to try to match the tourist dollars being brought to bitter local rival, Qatar, when they host the 2022 World Cup.

Only one project has not taken off the way Sheikh Mohamed wanted it to: his plans to build The World, a group of man-made islands in the Arabian Sea, with each island representing a country in the world. Unfortunately, this grandiose project was mis-timed, as it coincided with the credit crunch of 2008, which hit Dubai hard. Only a very small part of The World has been built thus far—in fact, only one island/country.

Aside from constructing tall buildings, flinging foreigners and local political dissidents into jail on the flimsiest of grounds using the state machinery, building cyber surveillance technology to spy on his own citizens, and purchasing Western arms to commit war crimes in Yemen (more about all this to come), Sheikh Mohamed's next greatest passion is horses. He has heavily invested in racehorses both at home and in the UK, and he is often seen in a three-piece suit and bowler hat hobnobbing with the UK's elite and aristocrats at the big races in that country, where his own horses run. The disgruntled members of his local society call this a love for *ghora*s (horses) and *goras* (white people).

A modern-day King, Sheikh Mohamed is active on social media as mentioned earlier. On the 2017 International Women's Day, he issued the following statement on LinkedIn: "Tomorrow we celebrate International Women's Day. In the UAE we are proud to recognize them for their inspiration and great contributions. Most of my team are women. I thank them— and call on every government minister and leader tomorrow to celebrate their female team members!"

Yet at the same time that he, the prime minister of the UAE, was offering these inspirational thoughts on social media, his political and social peers in Abu Dhabi were busy locking up Ukrainian Iryna Nohai (whose case we will discuss later), age twenty-seven, for being a *sharmuda* (prostitute), which simply meant that she had been having sex before marriage.

Like all Sheikhs in the emirates, Sheikh Mohamed lives in a palace facing the warm Arabian Sea. Many people say that the reason all the sheikhs' palaces face the ocean is should there ever be a coup or mass uprising in the UAE, the sheikhs and their immediate families would then be able to quickly leave the country on speedboats from their own backdoors.

Of course, even as the sheikhs and their close family members continue to look after the country's oil wealth, which is nearly entirely concentrated in Abu Dhabi, it is alleged that they keep most of the nation's wealth overseas, in places like Switzerland, and invested in gold, hard currencies, treasury bonds, and investments in blue-chip firms based in the Western hemisphere, which shows some wise decision-making. The UK, EU, USA, Japan, and the rest of the developed world can rest assured that if these rulers were ever to be kicked out of their country by their own people and turned into political refugees, they would not exactly have to rely on the refugee benefit systems in the West. These dictators already have their retirement nest eggs in place.

By now, it should be clear to my readers that it is very difficult to obtain any reliable information about the UAE's ruling families, including that of Dubai. Everything I have reported above, I learned through painstaking research, personal interviews, and experience. But good things happen to those who wait, and just before this book went into its final edit, a very mysterious YouTube video appeared, which could potentially yield a great deal more information.[1]

The video was recorded by a young woman who claims to be one of Sheikh Mohammed's daughters. In the video, the thirty-two-year-old Sheikha Latifa, a child of one of the shiekh's lesser-known six wives, explains that she escaped from Dubai because she did not have the most basic personal freedoms.

---

1. The video can be found here: www.msn.com/en-gb/news/world/runaway-princess-daughter-of-dubai-ruler-missing-after-posting-chilling-last-video-on-youtube/ar-BBKkbYY?li=AAnZ

She describes how she was held in prison for three years after a previous escape attempt. She is not allowed to drive or even travel to other emirates within the UAE, and she plans to seek political asylum in the United States. I cannot confirm the authenticity of this video one way or another, and it is under a great deal of scrutiny by numerous human rights organizations. However, Sheikha Latifa has reportedly disappeared since releasing this video.

Despite how common disappearances of local political dissidents and the detention of foreigners are, the UAE is a peaceful nation. A large part of this is due to the fact that the sheikhs want to remain in power, especially in the wake of the Arab Spring, when so many other rulers in the region were toppled, so they make every effort to keep the local population happy and pacified. Their biggest priority is to keep the money flowing into the pockets of their citizens and push a culture of consumption to keep them occupied. The result is a society that primarily values flashy possessions, luxury cars, good food, and holidays abroad.

For example, the life of even the average UAE soldier based in Dubai involves regularly racing from Dubai to Abu Dhabi at breakneck speeds in their high-performance cars in the morning for training and then racing back to Dubai in mid-afternoon even faster.

It's worth noting that the UAE is investing billions of dollars in Elon Musk's super-fast, super-cool hyperloop train system to ensure that people can get to Abu Dhabi from Dubai in a mere twelve minutes. Anyone who has ever lived in that country and has witnessed the maniacal speeds at which most locals drive on the Dubai-to-Abu Dhabi highway will seriously wonder why the government is wasting this money on a speedier transport system.

The reason for the soldiers' breakneck speeds between these two emirates is not always related to national security; it is generally for personal reasons, such as the need to sign personal loan documents before banks close for the day at two in the afternoon. After that, most of them—like many of their fellow countrymen—focus on their own business matters, which often involves sponsoring foreigners to supplement their meagre two-Mercedes-per-household lifestyle. However, this changed somewhat when regional power Saudi Arabia started entertaining territorial ambitions again, and these soldiers had to actually fight.

The UAE has never been a military superpower, nor has it ever pretended to be one. It is a peace-loving, business-oriented nation. During the early '90s, when the Iraqi dictator Saddam Hussein was creating tension in the Gulf region by occupying Kuwait, the joke in the Dubai expat community was: "Saddam has taken Kuwait City by night, will take Bahrain by breakfast, and Dubai by fax."

In the past, the life of a UAE soldier was a comfortable one with a fantastic salary and few actual military duties. However, this changed in 2015 when Saudi Arabia started to flex its muscles in the region and dragged the UAE into a sectarian civil war in Yemen. As of the date of this writing, several hundred UAE soldiers have been killed. In fact, the UAE has lost more soldiers in this current, covert war than it did in the past two Gulf Wars *combined*.

To be fair to the UAE, it has done a great deal to reduce the burden of this war on its citizens. It has reportedly hired Latin American mercenaries to fight—even offering them to pay in US dollars—rather than sending its own troops into battle. It has officially declared that its role in Yemen is over and gifted tanks to the pro-government forces they have been supporting so they can fight their own battles.[2] However, on June 13, 2018, it coordinated with Saudi Arabian forces to attack the Yemeni port city of Hodeidah.[3]

As with any war, this conflict is also costly on a financial level, and it comes at a time when oil prices are depressed (but being artificially tampered with, as of this writing), which negatively affects the economies of both proactive warmongers: the UAE and Saudi Arabia. Furthermore, the UAE has a substantial number of ethnic Yemeni locals. In fact, a large number of the police force's junior members are Yemeni. The UAE is, in many ways, a police state, and it relies heavily on its police force to maintain the "social harmony" it promotes as part of its international branding. What would happen if members of that same police force become agitated about the UAE's involvement in a war

---

2. You can read more here: https://uk.news.yahoo.com/uae-sending-colombian-mercenaries-yemen-sources-061321207.html

3. You can read more about it here: https://edition.cnn.com/2018/06/13/middleeast/yemen-hodeidah-attack-intl/index.html.

that is leading to the death of innocent Yemeni civilians? As of mid-2018, Saudi Arabians have terminated the employment contracts of 800,000 Yemenis in their country and deporting them back home, where they are being welcomed with open arms by the Houthi anti-government rebels, who are fighting the Saudi and UAE armed forces. This has also created a hiring crisis in Saudi Arabia, as young Saudi men and women are not accustomed to and do not want to work more than half a day.[4] Could similarly harsh treatment of Yemenis in Dubai further swell the ranks of the rebels the UAE is fighting and harm Dubai's economy?

In addition, Iran supports the Houthi rebels, and Dubai is also home to a large number of Iranians. Iran is also a very important trading partner for Dubai and has been for many generations.

In short, war in general, and this war in particular, is not good for Dubai's economy and international branding efforts, which are focused on stability, peace, and prosperity.

It is alleged that Dubai's trading volume increases whenever there are international sanctions against Iran, which does happen every so often.[5] In fact, Dubai's trading volume

---

4. You can read more here: www.msn.com/en-gb/news/world/yemen-civil-war-saudi-expulsion-of-yemeni-workers-swells-houthi-ranks/ar-BBK8cal?li=BBoPWjQ.

5. You can read more about Iran's financial relationship and trade through the UAE here: www.ft.com/content/2b174d9c-5c81-11e5-9846-de406ccb37f2.

increases whenever there is any kind of goods shortage in the Middle East and North Africa. This is because Dubai's staple business is based on exporting, importing, and re-exporting goods.

Chapter after chapter could be written on Iran's close economic association with Dubai. For our purposes, a single recent trade deal will suffice to illustrate how Dubai's free-trade economy regularly bypasses international sanctions. The credit for this information goes to the English-language financial blog, Zero Hedge, whose editors collectively write under the pseudonym "Tyler Durden," the name of a character from the novel and film *Fight Club*. In June 2014, "Durden" meticulously documented the following events.

Reza Zarrab, an Iranian-Turkish gold trader, used his network of companies, which were mainly based in Dubai, to trick US banks into processing transactions for Iran's benefit, despite international sanctions against the country. On paper, Zarrab's companies were sending thousands of tons of overpriced food to Iran from Dubai. What was actually flowing was gold from Turkey to Iran, via Dubai. The "goods" arrived in Dubai, shipping documents were changed, and then the "goods" were re-exported to Bandar Abbas, Iran's nearby port city.

It was a tidy operation until greed got in the way and brought the operation down. Mistakes and discrepancies showed up in the paperwork. In one case, the shipment was supposedly 150,000 tons of food, but the vessel hired to carry it was just 5,000 tons. In another instance, the goods that were supposedly being shipped were a large quantity of wheat, and the origin of the wheat was listed as Dubai. It was a bit of a stretch of the imagination to picture hot, desert-like Dubai producing much wheat at all, and eventually, the scam was uncovered. However, by then, an estimated US$12 billion-worth of gold had been shipped to Iran through Dubai.[6]

As far as Dubai is concerned, there is nothing wrong with this kind of business. No one cares about international sanctions against Iran, fictitious wheat, or illegal gold. "*Khalli walli* sanctions" is what they would say in Dubai at the first whiff of such grandiose sums of money. What matters in Dubai are things like whether Zarrab was paying his *arbab* (local UAE sponsor) on time, whether he was paying his rent for his villa in Jumeirah and his high-rise office in Deira, whether he had paid his Dubai municipality *shulka* (a form of municipality tax imposed on expats alone), whether any of his checks had bounced, and whether he was still faithfully paying his car loan for his Bentley. If all his financial commitments were being met, then Mr. Zarrab was deemed a good man. *Khalas*. End of story.

In many ways, the current conflict in Yemen is a de facto war between Iran and Saudi Arabia for regional dominance. As a result, Dubai's continued warm economic relationship with Iran when the UAE is at war with an Iranian-backed power is making Saudi Arabia, the other Big Brother in the region, very upset and nervous.

---

6. You can read the full article here: www.zerohedge.com/news/2014-06-25/turkeys-200-tons-secret-gold-trade-iran-biggest-most-bizarre-money-laundering-scheme

This regional political irritation is not going away any time soon. It is currently a small case of scabies, but if the UAE is not careful, what is equivalent to a minor skin irritation now could turn into a full-blown cancer of the internal organs. This war remains one of the biggest threats to doing business in Dubai, and in fact, Dubai's very existence could be threatened if this conflict is not settled soon. Furthermore, according to the business daily Economic Times (ET) Dubai thrived in the past by keeping cordial relations with all countries in the region and accepting investments and trades from all of them. Now that is becoming impossible as UAE, Saudi and all other countries in the area have cut off all economic relations with Qatar, thereby ending Dubai's role as a business base for super rich Qatar.

Now that you have a basic understanding of Dubai's place in the world, let's move away from the bigger picture and into some finer details about life in Dubai.

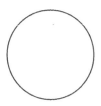

THE TRUE GUIDING LIGHT OF DUBAI: MONEY

The very creation, existence, survival, and growth of Dubai is only ever about one thing: *money.*

The true guiding spirit of Dubai is *fulus*, the local word for "money." "Sheikh *Fulus*" is the true lord of the emirate. Nothing else matters (other than *wasta*, which we will discuss below), and nothing else ever will. Everybody in Dubai—locals, expats, sheikhs, and labourers—are all in one business: the business of making *fulus*. A popular saying is, "*Mahad fulus, mafi* happiness," or "No money, no happiness."

Of course, to be fair to Dubai, money is important for everyone, everywhere in the world. There is nothing wrong with chasing money. But in Dubai, that is the only thing anyone ever chases.

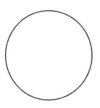

WASTA-OLOGY

If "Sheikh *Fulus*" is the lifeblood of Dubai, *wasta* is the heart, which facilitates the mobility and circulation of Dubai's lifeblood. The concept of *wasta* better summarizes Dubai than many thousands of other words strung together.

Very simply, *wasta* translates to "influence" or "contacts" in Northern Emirati Arabic. It is the concept of "It's not what you know, but who you know." However, to suggest that *wasta* merely means "influence," we are practically insulting this sacrosanct concept that holds the whole of Dubai together. *Wasta* runs through all of Dubai's veins, and it is what fuelled its enormous growth over the years.

To be fair to Dubai, every single country and society in the world has its own indigenous form of *wasta* that helps individuals of a certain class skirt the law. England has its networks of relationships through elite private gentlemen's clubs. In America, there is a longstanding "pay to play" culture, in which money buys access to everything, especially politics. Fraternal orders such as the Freemasons are common throughout the Western world, and it is said that their members are often top judges, politicians, doctors, and lawyers who would do anything to protect their brethren.

In India, a version of *wasta* is widely known as "back-door," a system of favoritism and nepotism, which often results in undeserving candidates landing plum jobs and promotions ahead of truly deserving and qualified individuals, simply because of their connections. In India, "back-door" is used not only to secure jobs, but also to influence the outcomes of major commercial bids in both the public and private sectors. The instances of such misdeeds are endless.

But these are all very crude and obvious forms of corruption, without any of the style or finesse found in Dubai's *wasta* concept. In addition, these are also confined to a certain cross-section of society, whereas *wasta* involves everyone and everything in Dubai. It is very deeply embedded in the culture and extremely effective when used to achieve a certain outcome. It combines the best and worst aspects of India's "back-door," British "influence," American "pay to play," and the general Western "art of Freemasonry," all nicely wrapped up in a convenient, easy-to-use package.

Wasta is not just about money and corruption. Yes, money plays an important role because it generates the power to seek or provide *wasta*, but money is not the entire focus of this concept. Friendship, returning favors, making connections, generating goodwill, and a host of other factors all beautifully mingle to create the most powerful tool to survive and thrive in Dubai. *Wasta* is not just a practice; it is a way of life for both expats and locals alike.

Of course, *wasta* only works for foreigners up to a point. Say an expatriate businessman has derived a certain level of *wasta* through his prominent local sponsor, and he feels that this makes him powerful in Dubai. Soon after, he realizes that another business, also run by an expatriate, is not honoring a large payment that is overdue. That business's sponsor is far more powerful than his, so this second business has even more *wasta*. When the smaller businessman tries to get them to pay their dues, the larger business owner is annoyed; due to their greater *wasta*, they feel justified in not paying. They refer the matter to their more powerful local sponsor, who brings it to the attention of the first businessman's less-powerful local sponsor.

Suddenly, the local with less *wasta* will no longer take calls from the businessman he has been sponsoring for years. When they do communicate, the local says, "Everyone is saying that you are not a good man. I do not want to sponsor a bad man."

This businessman has been religiously meeting his commitments for ten years, entertaining his local sponsor with expensive dinners in the best restaurants in Dubai, and catering to his every whim and fancy over and above the extortionate sponsorship fees, all so that he can visit his sponsor's office a couple of times every year, sign a few visa forms, and continue operating his business in Dubai. Yet now, all of a sudden, he is dubbed "a bad man?" How? Why?

In short, the local with more *wasta* used his influence to help his own expat client avoid making a large, legitimate payment in order to pad the business's bottom line and, thus, line his own pockets. The local with less *wasta* suffered for it, and so he passed his displeasure on to his own expat client.

One of the most important unwritten laws of *wasta* is that no matter how strong a relationship is between a local sponsor and his expat client, no matter how long they have known each other, two locals will never fight over an expat. They will readily sacrifice the expat, rather than fight with each other. This is due to a very simple philosophy: "All of these foreigners will eventually go home, but we locals have to live here with each other. We cannot kill each other over these foreigners."

Wasta directly impacts life for all residents of Dubai, especially when it comes to dealing with law enforcement. Having a great deal of *wasta* can ease interactions with the law; having little or none can make it extremely difficult.

Consider what happened to Romit Ahuja, an Indian banker in Dubai with a great deal of *wasta* due to his excellent networking skills. In a personal interview, he told me how he had a good salary and was thus able to bring his family over to Dubai. Surya, his wife, immediately demanded that they get a maid from India because she could not stand doing housework.

Surya had a harsh, sharp temper and a proclivity for violence even toward her husband when she was angry. Her husband knew she was a volatile person who had no qualms about hurting those she felt were below her in the social strata. However, for the sake of their children, he went along with her demands and sponsored a girl, no more than ten or twelve years old, from a village near their home in India to be their household help in Dubai.

The girl's parents were overjoyed at the prospect of their daughter going to Dubai to earn some "foreign cash." They were confident that she would send her entire salary back home to them because she would be well provided for by her Indian "family" in Dubai. Yet as soon as she arrived in Dubai, she was almost immediately subjected to Surya's verbal lashings. These soon turned into severe beatings, and the little girl was often completely covered in dark bruises.

Unable to take the physical torture anymore, one evening, the little girl ran out of the house in sheer desperation. A Dubai police patrol car picked her up and took her to their nearest station, the Al Murragabat station in Deira. The officers called her sponsor, Mr. Ahuja, and asked him to come down to the police station right away. Being an intelligent and a streetwise man, he immediately knew that his wife was in deep trouble. So, before he and his wife left for the station, he called a friend who was an IT officer in a local government bank who knew and regularly worked with some of the police officers in that particular station and asked him to accompany them.

When the trio arrived at the station, the police were already writing up an official case against the sponsoring couple because they had very quickly identified the effects of child abuse and slavery. They were clearly angry about the situation and were actively encouraging the young girl to lodge a case against her sponsors. But once the officers saw Ahuja's friend, whom they dealt with on a regular basis, they immediately changed their tone. With little effort on the sponsors' part, the police quickly shut down the case entirely.

Ahuja learned later that the policemen were returning a favour to his friend. Like most junior employees in the world, many of these policemen would run out of money before their next paycheck came through. Since the police salaries went through his bank, this friend was able to use his position as a bank officer to give these men an advance on their salaries to get them through until their next paycheck. Thus, this man had secured considerable *wasta* with the police, and he used it to get his friend and his wife off the hook, even if it meant a tragic, heart-rending, and very real complaint about child abuse was never investigated.

Thankfully, Ahuja had the sense to recognize that if he kept this small girl at their Dubai home any longer, they would soon have blood on their hands, which may well lead to the firing squad for both husband and wife. As the girl's sponsor, he quickly canceled her residence visa and sent her back home to India. It was the end of another Dubai dream, but it also helped get a vulnerable young girl out of harm's way.

Another serious crime in Dubai is sex outside of marriage. If a couple is caught living together without a proper marriage certificate, they are immediately taken into police custody. The woman is forced to undergo an intrusive medical examination by forensically trained police doctors to check for evidence of an active sex life, and then both parties are taken to court and sentenced to jail time. After they have served their sentences, they are immediately deported. There is no chance of appeal, regardless of previous good behavior, this being a first-time 'offence', a record of investments or job creation in the country, or any other positive mitigating circumstances. However, this nightmare situation is only for people without *wasta*. For those with considerable *wasta*, the same crime is handled quite differently.

Recently, a very well-known international footballer that was employed as a coach for a Dubai football team had a difference of opinion with his girlfriend. The woman became so angry that she went berserk, left their home, and started to harass him. Despite all rational pleas, including generous offers of a monetary settlement, nothing could placate this woman, and the footballer felt that he had no other options except to go to the police and seek some help.

Despite having scored many goals in the past against some very tough opponents, he was not at all prepared for what happened next. Having gone to the police with the simple request of getting help to calm his irate girlfriend, the footballer was shocked when the first thing they did was demand to see a marriage certificate for the couple.

Fortunately for him and for his girlfriend, this international footballer had a great deal of *wasta*, and once the police understood who he was, all concerns about a marriage certificate were dropped. Due to his *wasta*, he was able to get away with what would have led to immediate imprisonment and summary deportation for most other foreign residents of the UAE.

In contrast, a very similar "crime" was recently committed

by ordinary residents of Dubai/UAE with considerably less *wasta* and with very different results. In the spring of 2017, Ukrainian Iryna Nohai, age twenty-seven, and her South African boyfriend, Emlyn Culverwell, age twenty-nine, were arrested in an Abu Dhabi hospital after doctors discovered that Nohai was pregnant when she came in complaining about severe stomach cramps. Because they were unmarried, the medical staff reported the couple to the authorities, and they were arrested on the spot. The couple had violated the United Arab Emirates' morality laws, which mandate that sex outside marriage is a punishable crime. They were both denied bail, as well as any state-appointed legal representation, and their friends and family desperately scrambled to hire an overpriced attorney. The couple even asked to be married in prison, but the judge denied their request.[7]

This is not an uncommon situation for women on the lowest rung of UAE society, such as the Sri Lankan, Filipino, or sub-Saharan African women who work as household help. They often strike up a relationship with a man, and if by chance they fall pregnant, there is no escape for them back to their homelands, since their sponsors hold their passports. When they are discovered, they are immediately thrown into prison,

---

7. You can read more about this case here: www.independent.co.uk/news/world/middle-east/couple-detained-uae-sex-outside-of-marriage-south-africa-ukraine-abu-dhabi-a7619201.html.

where they end up giving birth.[8]

But what happens next? What happens to those "illegitimate" babies? Are they allowed to remain with their imprisoned, unwed mothers? Are they given away to childless UAE women from influential families? The sad fact is that no one knows.

The only times *wasta* fails is when there is a case of a returned check or a murder with ample evidence and witnesses. In such instances, even if the Dubai Police want and try to help the accused, it cannot. Even *wasta* has its limits.

---

8. You can read the story of a woman who recently gave birth outside of wedlock in Dubai here: www.independent.co.uk/news/world/middle-east/woman-arrested-for-giving-birth-to-illegitimate-baby-in-uae-a7493016.html.

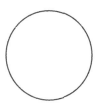

DOING BUSINESS IN DUBAI: THE VISA

Every year, millions of people (fourteen million in 2017 alone, if Dubai's official figures are to be believed) head to Dubai for tourism, a high-salary tax-free career, or step out of their comfort zones to explore new business opportunities. Thousands of expats already live in Dubai and are excited by its super-entrepreneurial environment. But no matter what draws foreigners to Dubai, there is one thing they all need: a visa.

The visa business is possibly one of the biggest money-makers for the Dubai government and its locals. Traditionally, there are three types of visas in Dubai:

1. **Transit Visas**: These are primarily issued by hotels to tourists, and they are valid for fourteen or fifteen days. Business firms can also issue transit visas for things like

inviting international partners to Dubai for negotiations.

This type of visa is normally available at the airport upon arrival, and they are held at the customer-service desk just before immigration/passport control. The sponsoring firm or hotel also usually faxes or emails a copy to the visitor in advance, just in case there is any confusion or mix-up at the airport.

As of 2018, visitors from some countries can now get their visas online. However, the website that details this process is only in English and can be very confusing. No matter where you are from, it is essential to read your nation's visa requirements very carefully before boarding your flight to the UAE.[9]

All tourists, especially those coming from developing nations, must be warned that they can expect very rude behaviour and treatment from local immigration officers. In addition, it is essential to know exactly when your visa expires—down to the exact hour. Arriving at the Dubai airport to return home after a holiday with an expired visa—even if just by a few hours—can earn one an immediate fine and very rude treatment from the immigration officers on duty, who will not hold back in letting you know who the real masters in that country

9. You can read more about the current electronic visa applications here. No matter what kind of visa you are interested in, please read the details on this site very carefully: www.emirates.com/english/before-you-fly/visa-passport-information/uae-visas/.

are.

Transit visas can be purchased for as little as few hundred dirhams a piece, but the price does vary. In the past, transit visas could be very expensive for single, unaccompanied women, but less expensive for men. Prices also vary depending on which country the individual is from, when it is being purchased, who is issuing the transit visa (for example, whether it is through a business firm or a hotel), and a host of other factors. Always make sure to be very clear about your personal requirements and situation when securing your visa and before you land in Dubai.

Foreigners who are changing jobs in Dubai also use this kind of visa. If an expat leaves their job or is sacked, their current employer immediately cancels their residence visa. Because their passport must show an immigration exit stamp before they can secure a new residency visa, most Dubai residents who are changing jobs procure a transit visa and head over to Qatar(not these days, as we understand!), Bahrain, or Oman, all about a forty-five-minute flight away. They then return to Dubai on the same aircraft and come back into Dubai with a transit visa. Then, they just have to go through the formalities of organizing another residence visa.

2. **Visit Visas**: These are the second-most common type of visa in Dubai. They allow a person to stay in Dubai for up to ninety days, plus an additional ten-day grace period. Some are issued for a solid ninety days, while others

must be renewed every thirty days or so, depending on who is issuing and purchasing the visa. This type of visa is often used by elderly parents visiting their children for an extended period, individuals who are looking for employment in Dubai and need to be present in the country for a while to attend job interviews, and those who are trying to set up a business and carry out initial market research.

These visas are far more expensive than transit visas, though, again, the price depends on who is purchasing the visa, where they're purchasing it from, and even why they are purchasing it. Like the transit visa, these can be particularly expensive for single, unaccompanied women, because it is assumed that the woman is coming into the country to pursue a rather dubious—and illegal—line of work. Hence, the premium on visas for single woman is supposed to make it more difficult for them to enter the country.

3. **Residence Visas**: As the name suggests, this type of visa is for foreigners who are actively employed and reside in Dubai. These used to be good for three years, but they have recently been reduced to only two years, except for the employees of some government departments, who are still allowed to have three-year residence visas.

Having a residence visa does not guarantee that the holder's family can join him in Dubai. There is a minimum income threshold that must be met before a man (and yes, it is mostly men) is allowed to sponsor his family. The family can only come in if the man who is the employee,sponsors his family.The family cannot come in on their own rights unless they are sponsored for visa purposes. No one knows exactly what this income threshold is, and if the man has enough *wasta*, he can easily skirt the income-threshold requirement.

Once a residence visa is issued, the holder can immediately open a bank account, take out loans, and apply for a credit card or car loan in Dubai. However, the moment a person loses their job, the residence visa is canceled, and the banks are made aware of this fact. If the person has any outstanding financial obligations, they will be put on a "black list," which prevents them from leaving the country. This is a sadly common occurrence in Dubai.

Slowly but surely, there is a fourth type of visa that is beginning to emerge in the UAE: the investor's visa. The UAE has many Free-Trade Zones, like the Jebel Ali Free-Trade Zone on the outskirts of Dubai, and many of these Zones are now issuing these "investor's resident visas."

Free-Trade Zones are areas where goods can be landed, handled, manufactured or reconfigured, and re-exported without the intervention of customs authorities. They are also designated areas in which companies are taxed very lightly or not at all in order to encourage economic activity. Of course, since the UAE, and Dubai in particular, pride themselves on being tax-free and duty-free, why do they need to have such designated Free-Trade Zones? It comes down to sponsorship and visas.

In the UAE, you need a local sponsor in order to operate a business, and with that comes the possibility of human greed. This has made many businesses and foreign investors wary of coming to the UAE, so the government set up these Free-Trade Zones to address the problem and try to woo investors, telling them that they can have complete control over and ownership of their business and do not need a sponsor. In these Free-Trade Zones, all sponsorship and visa functions are run through their respective regional authorities with pre-determined fixed rates. This way, foreign businesses can avoid any kind of personal interference from a local sponsor, though they should be aware of potential rate hikes each year and other hidden costs. More and more Free-Trade Zones are being opened because Saudi Arabia, which is opening up its economy to foreign investments, and Qatar which is following suit, are starting to negatively impact Dubai's foreign investments.

One example of a popular Free-Trade Zone near Dubai is the Dubai International Financial Centre (DIFC), which is the go-to destination for foreign investors in the financial services sector. It was set up in 2004 and boasts its own courts, delivers everything in English, and promises zero interference from locals.[10] Due to this zone's transparency, you can even consult its online business database, which details how many firms have made DIFC their base of operations since 2004, how many

---

10. You can read more about it here: www.difc.ae/.

firms have since been dissolved, and even if any "big fish" global conglomerates have pulled out of the DIFC.[11]

To get these investor's visas, individuals often open small businesses and rent a virtual office and post-office box in one of the Free-Trade Zones and then operate their business out of their flat in Dubai. This is not strictly legal, as a foreigner needs to have a sponsorship from a Dubai local in order to operate a business in Dubai, but the laws are murky and ever changing at best, and so long as a local with a fair amount of *wasta* does not go after the "offender," it is easy to get away with such petty "crimes" in highly entrepreneurial Dubai.

Many wealthy, employed expat men whose "time is up," which occurs when they turn sixty years old, remain in the UAE by purchasing these investor's visas and pretend to be entrepreneurs. These individuals have grown too accustomed to the UAE's high-quality roads, cars, food, and other luxuries and do not want to return to their home countries where such things cannot measure up. And so, they remain in the desert, burning through their lifesavings on visas and overpriced rental accommodations.

---

11. The database is listed in alphabetical order: www.difc.ae/public-register.

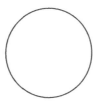

SPONSORSHIP IN DUBAI

Of course, when most businesses set up shop in Dubai and send employees there, they choose to go to locals for sponsorship. This offers "the personal touch" and allows foreigners to connect with someone on the ground with an existing network of connections. It is the sponsor's job to get all the necessary licenses from Dubai's Economic Department, get the Labor Department to conduct the inspection of the business premises, and most importantly, organize the visas.

There are several important factors to keep in mind regarding this very important part of setting up a business in Dubai. First of all, only UAE locals or GCC nationals can sponsor expats. Any other Arab-speaking person wearing the local outfit cannot be a sponsor. Anyone considering a potential sponsor should make sure that they have very positive references before even starting a conversation about sponsorship. Dubai's grapevine is more powerful than the best Google search, so get as much information on a person as possible. There is very little official information on locals in Dubai, so it is very common to rely on word-of-mouth, rumours, and hearsay in Dubai. Some large organizations in Dubai even have formal "researchers," whose job is to find out as much as they can about a person or a business through the local grapevine.

Some locals are full-time professional sponsors and make a good living simply by sponsoring between fifteen and twenty—if not more—foreign businesses at a time. Many others also hold down day jobs and just sponsor a small handful of businesses.

How much a Dubai sponsorship costs will depend on the sponsoring local's reputation, power, and of course, his perceived *wasta*. A powerful local could be what's known as a "local local"—a member of the traditional local Arab society—and/or someone with a senior position in the Immigration Department, the police, the Labour Department, local banks, or even the ruler's /sheikh's private office. Distant cousins of the sheikh or his family could be defined as particularly powerful locals, so long as they can prove their connection to the royal family.

The price of a local Dubai sponsorship can range between Dhs 35,000 and Dhs 500,000 per annum, though it can be much, much higher. There is no set fee, and prices are decided on a case-by-case basis and paid *upfront* every year irrespective of the performance of an existing business and even before a new business makes a single dollar in terms of revenue. That does generate a question or two about Dubai's tax free claims. Also taxation in any economy is a rear ended payment but Dubai's sponsorship fees are payable upfront only. Apart from the initial sponsorship fees, the sponsored expat also needs to throw in little sweeteners, or what is known as *bakshish* in Arabic, for the sponsor from time to time. This often takes the form of the sponsor approaching his client with a request for a "favor," such as, "My daughter needs an operation in London; could we get the air tickets from your firm, please?" or "I am buying a second car for my third wife; could the firm pick up the loan? I will charge you a little less money next year to renew your visa"—which, of course, would not actually happen.

Once a local is chosen as a potential sponsor and the businessman has had an initial phone call with him, it is important to set up a face-to-face meeting. This will often be held at the local's office, in the reception area of a glitzy hotel, or perhaps even at the airport, especially if the local is an immigration officer.

At this meeting, it is very important to make sure that the potential sponsor is a local with a UAE passport, and is not an expat Arab. However, this must be done subtly and without directly asking. In addition, do not try to get too familiar with the potential sponsor at this meeting. Do not ask about the local's family and do not attempt the local-to-local greeting of rubbing noses. Once the initial pleasantries are over, the conversation will go something like this:

Expat: Can we get five residence visas for this licensed business?

Local Sponsor: No problem, no problem at all! *Mafi mushkil*!

I know the Head of Immigration very well, and my assistant knows the Head of the Visa Section very well.

Expat: Can you help me get a bank account?

Local: How much will you deposit initially? [This question is meant to determine the expat's liquidity.] No problem! I know all the managers(*mudirs*) at Bank Emirate al Daulia on Maktoum Road and Fish Roundabout. They are my friends; we go to the same bodybuilding association, so no problem at all.

Expat: Can you organize the Labor Department check?

Local: Of course, no problem! *Mafi Mushkil*. The Labour Head for Deira, Dubai is my ex-colleague; we used to work at the Dubai airport together a few years ago.

It will go on and on, like this. Everything is "no problem." The potential sponsor knows everyone, can get everything done. There is happiness and smiles all round. The local will assure the expat again and again, "Do not worry. I am your brother; you are my brother. In Dubai, no one can touch you. Just relax, *habibi*. I am there for you."

Then, of course, comes the small matter of money. The sponsor will give a verbal invoice, which, of course, will increase over time and will not take into account the *bakshish* that will be expected in the future.

Apart from the sponsorship fees, which are a major factor in choosing a local sponsor, different businesses have different needs, which can also impact what sort of sponsor they need. For example, if the business in question is in the hospitality industry and will need to be able to issue a large volume of visas for both its customers and its employees, then it would be highly advisable for that business to get a very senior person in the Immigration Department as a sponsor, as they would be well-positioned to help facilitate this.

The expatriate business will also need to decide whether they want a "small," non-interfering local who will accept a smaller sponsorship fee and just handle routine requests, or a powerful local who can take care of everything through his *wasta*. It must be remembered that a powerful local can also be very interfering and, unlike a "small" local, can start asking questions that are, in reality, gross meddling.

Of course, we cannot paint all locals with the same brush. There are locals who, for decades on end, do not even show their faces on the business premises so long as they get their annual sponsorship fees. These individuals will simply say, "Send the papers to my office, and I will do what is needed."

On a somewhat lighter a note, it is important that whatever kind of car you drive in Dubai, make sure that it is a cheaper and a smaller model than what your local sponsor drives. In a car-proud society like Dubai's, driving a nicer car than your sponsor can quickly lead to much higher annual sponsorship fees the following year.

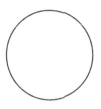

DUBAI'S ECONOMY

While it is in a part of the world associated with oil wealth, Dubai's economy is not outwardly dependant on it. Dubai has very little fossil fuel resources of its own, and whatever oil reserves it did have, have been diligently pumped out over the years. No new oilfields have been discovered in the emirate of Dubai, so almost all oil reserves—and hence, oil wealth—in the UAE are in the hands of Abu Dhabi, the richest emirate and the capital of the UAE.

So what are Dubai's primary commercial activities, and where do its opulent buildings and hotels come from? Dubai is a trading-based economy and a highly successful entrepôt. Its main business is import and re-export, a very simple business model. An Indian expression brilliantly summarizes Dubai's core business competence: "Goods from here to there, and goods from there to here." Billions of dollars' worth of goods pass through Dubai every hour, every day, every week, every month, and every year, sometimes without even touching Dubai's shore.

Dubai's business model works particularly well if there are trade restrictions in place, especially for large neighboring economies, like India and Iran. For example, for many decades, India had severe import restrictions in order to shore up its foreign exchange reserves, and Dubai was an ideal place to bypass these. Iran always seems to have some sort of trade embargo imposed by the Western powers, but it easily bypasses these by going through Dubai.

However, with import restrictions easing all over the world thanks to globalization, there is a dwindling need for third-party shipping bases like Dubai. Of course, there are still plenty of places facing a shortage of goods due to war, drought, and famine, and Dubai's free-trade attitude and easy access to goods does help in these situations.

Still, over the years, the government of Dubai has been desperately trying to diversify its economy. They came up with the idea of building up the desert and then selling it off, a classic "If you build it, they will come" mentality. Thus began one of the most lucrative business models in Dubai's economic history: property development.

Until the early part of the new millennium, foreigners were not allowed to buy property in the UAE, and property ownership was the exclusive privilege of the locals, nationals of other Gulf countries and some expat Arabs. Now it seems, anyone with the money can own property in Dubai but please check this point out very carefully before investing in Dubai property because it is said ownership restrictions still exist for parts of Dubai. Unfortunately, this effort nearly bombed with the property crash of 2008.

Today, the majority of Dubai's property investments are from wealthy AGCC nationals—those from Saudi Arabia, Kuwait, Qatar, etc.—and their family businesses. For these individuals, Dubai is like a breath of fresh air in the stiflingly restrictive atmosphere of the Gulf. Dubai is their Las Vegas and their Monaco. Compared to what they are used to at home, there are no apparent restrictions for them in Dubai. There is plenty of alcohol in the restaurants without any restrictions—you don't need police clearance to drink in restaurants in Dubai. For the wealthy, it is a great place to meet "friends with benefits" of the opposite sex. Plus, for them, it is close to home.

In short, a significant portion of the investments coming into Dubai in the form of buying property are from its oil-rich capital, Abu Dhabi, and the other oil-based economies in the region. In reality, the idea that Dubai does not depend on the oil industry is simply another myth.

Oil prices were a heady US$120 per barrel in July 2014, but by December 2017, it was about US$62 per barrel, after having slipped precipitately to around US$25 per barrel in early 2016. As of this writing in June 2018, it is hovering in the mid-US$70s. Before this crash, the Gulf economies, especially that of local Big Brother Saudi Arabia, were basking in the glory of high oil prices, which were good for social cohesion, something the Gulf governments all needed in the wake of the Arab Spring a few years before.

Oil prices started their downward spiral in mid-2014, due to the arrival of a new, disruptive oil-extraction technology, fracking, which has created an abundant supply of what is now known as US shale oil or tight oil. As of mid-2018, the US is producing more than ten million barrels of oil per day, which is equivalent to adding another country like Qatar to the global oil supply equation. This excess supply has caused oil prices to plummet, and that has had an almost devastating impact on the AGCC countries and their economies, including the UAE.

Furthermore, the world is falling out of love with fossil fuels, due to their impact on the global climate changes. Elon Musk's electric cars are on the horizon for many, and they are not going to boost demand for oil. The car-sharing company, Uber, is also expected to severely weaken demand for global oil, as more and more people share car rides. In fact, Saudi Arabia is reportedly more afraid of Uber than it is of US shale oil.

All the countries in the region—from the mighty Saudi Arabia to the humble Bahrain and Oman—are cutting subsidies for their residents on things like water, gas, and electricity as a result of falling oil prices, which drives up the cost of living. Governments throughout the region are slashing investments and backing away from mega-development projects, translating to the elimination of thousands of jobs in the region. All of this means less disposable income in the pockets of Gulf nationals.

When talking about oil prices in the region, we also need to take into consideration the break-even point for various nations' governments. Depending on their expenses and social commitments to their citizens, each country in the region has a different break-even point for oil prices. These social commitments are especially important in the wake of the Arab Spring; individual governments are keen to meet their commitments to their local population so as to keep them happy or risk another backlash.

Kuwait has the lowest break-even point for a barrel of oil at US$58. Saudi Arabia has the highest at around US$90 to US$100 per barrel, though they also have the lowest cost to extract a barrel of oil. Lavish salaries and benefits for Saudi citizens constitute a major part of that government's expenses, which is a large part of what pushes up the break-even price of their oil. While there are no official figures, the UAE's break-even point for a barrel of oil is estimated to be anywhere between US$71 and US$81per barrel. Although the UAE has some of the lowest oil production costs in the whole world, like Saudi Arabia, the UAE has some significant social costs built into every barrel of oil.

With oil prices below the UAE's break-even point, there is tremendous pressure on even Abu Dhabi's and Dubai's current liquidity, despite the fact that both Emirates have substantial foreign reserves of around a trillion dollars held in investible assets all around the world. Even its flagship investment fund, Abu Dhabi Investment Authority, closed its headquarters in London during 2016 and quietly left the city.

So yes, low oil prices can wreak havoc on any oil-based economy, and if these low oil prices continue, Dubai cannot expect to receive another ten billion dollar bailout from Abu

Dhabi, like they did in 2008 after the real estate market crash.

This is already having an effect on Dubai, the playground of the rich and cosmopolitan of the Gulf fraternity. Gulf nationals suddenly have less money to spend in Dubai's hotels, restaurants, and pubs. Travellers are downgrading from business and first class to economy class on flights through Dubai's flagship airline. Investments in real estate from Dubai's core investment population have slowed. Fewer Gulf nationals are opening new businesses in Dubai. Tourism in general is down, and there are reports that Saudi and Kuwaiti tourism to Dubai was down at least 60 percent in 2016. With a US$140 billion debt—which is 132 percent of Dubai's gross domestic product—and continued low oil prices, is it possible that another 2008-style economic slowdown is looming for Dubai? It is certainly possible.[12]

So even though Dubai itself does not have much in the way of oilfields, it is certainly reliant on the oil industry. Since July 2014 and the start of the oil-price plunge, thousands of jobs have been wiped out in Dubai. Countless expats have lost everything and were forced to return to their home countries with nothing. The downturn has been so bad that even some senior locals in Dubai have lost their highly lucrative jobs—a highly unusual turn of events and a rather dramatic sign of how bad things are.

However, the official reason for these senior locals being fired is quite different. In fact, many of the actual "You're fired" moments were staged. In several cases, there were dramatic

---

12. See more here: www.aljazeera.com/news/2015/02/dubai-debt-storm-clouds-gathering-150201075605951.html.

pictures and videos on television and social media of Dubai's ruler, Sheikh Mohamed, visiting government offices during their regular hours and finding no senior local managers present. This was summer, and these locals were, in all likelihood, on holiday in London or looking after their own businesses—both very normal practices in Dubai, as the sheikh knew. Despite that, he fired these big-fish locals on the spot and on camera to show the whole world that he means business. And, of course, the whole world saw this and applauded his commitment to professionalism.[13]

Of course, the whole world is not privy to what happens behind the scenes within Dubai's government. Sheikh Mohamed's private office, called the Ruler's Office, is the very heart of Dubai's government, and it houses some of its biggest enterprises. Jobs in this organization are considered jobs for life, but in the current vicious economic downturn, which started in 2014, even safe havens like these have not been spared. As multi-million dollar projects started getting shelved, the entire Events Department of a particular division was disbanded, leading to many job losses for locals.

Dubai also hosts a substantial services sector, dominated by Western multinational companies. With the economic downturn in the region, these companies have also laid off thousands of expat employees who have gone back to their

---

13. You can read more about this here: www.telegraph.co.uk/ news/2016/08/30/dubais-ruler-orders-management-shake-up-after-unannouced-inspect/.

home countries entirely or have sent their families back home and are trying to remain in the UAE with another job and a lower salary. All of this means there will be less expat spending in Dubai on housing, education, groceries, and in the shopping malls.

As a result of all this, Dubai is trying to diversify its economy. For one thing, it's trying to establish itself as *the* regional financial hub and has established a formal stock market. However, before investing in the Dubai Stock Exchange, potential investors need to do their research. If you are considering such an investment, ask questions such as:

1. How many stocks are listed in the market?
2. What is the total valuation and liquidity of the market?
3. What are the rules governing the stock market?
4. What is the licensing process for the operators?
5. Who are the stock market regulators?
6. What are the settlement processes?
7. What are the laws governing stock market regulations?

All investors should do their homework both on the markets themselves and the individual securities before putting their funds into this market. Can a free-enterprise concept such as a stock market truly operate in a police state like Dubai? Can the police and the civil authorities that regulate the stock market truly understand the concept that there can be both investment gains and losses and not lock up a genuine stockbroker if a local has lost money on the stock market or if a deal has bombed?

Another big focus for Dubai in recent years has been

its efforts to become a global healthcare destination. It has established the Dubai Healthcare City and a regulatory body called the Dubai Healthcare Authority (DHA). However, just as there are questions one must ask before investing in Dubai's stock market, there are questions one must ask before entrusting their medical care to the Dubai Healthcare Authority. These questions include:

1. What sorts of doctors with what sort of recognized qualifications are providing the care?

2. Are the authorities conducting an accurate assessment of these doctors' skills?

3. A question for the medical professionals themselves: will the doctors gain any professional credibility from their work in Dubai, or will they be sacrificing their careers for a few thousand tax-free dollars?

4. Do the patients have any means of redress in the event of a botched operation?

5. On the other hand, will the doctors be locked up based on a simple, single, and illegitimate complaint from a local or because a patient could not be revived, despite their best efforts?

6. What sort of language skills do these doctors have? Do they understand English? Do they have clear professional proficiency in Arabic? After all, the majority of the patients coming to Dubai will be from the AGCC countries that currently head to India, Malaysia, or if they can afford it, the West, for their medical needs.

There are always a lot of questions that need to be answered whenever Dubai launches a new enterprise. What is true for bankers, software engineers, dentists, architects, and stockbrokers is also true for doctors.

Dubai and its Gulf neighbors have also made themselves hubs for international flights. The three main Gulf airlines—Emirates Airline (Dubai), Etihad Airways (Abu Dhabi), and Qatar Airways (Doha)—have built massive airport infrastructures in their home cities, but the airline hub business is mainly concentrated in Dubai. Heavily subsidized by the state—to the tune of US$52 billion since 2004—these regional airlines are adding thousands of seats and, as the US airlines allege, completely misuse the Open Sky Policies, which call for the liberalization of the rules and regulations governing the international aviation industry in order to promote fair competition. This subsidized support includes interest-free government "loans" with no repayment obligation, government grants and capital injections, free land, airport fee exemptions, and, very importantly, the employees of these Gulf airlines are not allowed to form unions to represent their interests. By adding thousands of cheap airplane seats while receiving significant government subsidies, these airlines are doing the aviation equivalent of dumping manufactured goods. According to Oscar Munoz, the CEO of United Airlines, "Those airlines aren't airlines. They're international branding vehicles for their countries."

Before you book your cheap tickets on Dubai's flagship Emirates Airlines though, consider the way it can, and often does, treat its customers. Beth Evans, from Birmingham in the

UK, was flying Emirates Airlines to Dubai with her boyfriend when the crew overheard her mention to him that she was suffering from period pains shortly before take-off. The couple was thrown off the plane as a result. Apart from the personal embarrassment, they had to fork out extra money to continue on their holiday.[14]

In another case, Derek and Lesley Donaldson from Scotland could not travel to Dubai in February 2018 when their Emirates Airlines flight to Dubai was cancelled due to heavy snow. However, the airline still charged the couple £1600 for the cancelled flight.[15]

Having said all this, an Emirates Airlines flight, especially in the upper classes, is truly an extraordinary experience. Just hope you are lucky enough to avoid any "ground turbulence, Dubai-style."

In addition to all of these efforts to diversify its economy, Dubai is also billing itself as possibly the greatest tourist destination in that part of the world, which seems to be working, with one-and-a-half billion people falling over themselves to vacation there. Plus, Dubai and the UAE have encouraged investors to set up manufacturing operations in its many Free-Trade Zones and industrial areas, though it still has a long way to go before

---

14. You can read the full story here: www.independent.co.uk/travel/news-and-advice/woman-thrown-off-emirates-flight-period-pain-complaint-dubai-beth-evans-a8220836.html.

15. You can read the full story here: https://uk.style.yahoo.com/grounded-snow-owe-us-1-100238209.html.

it can compete with established players in that field, like China or Singapore. However before we move on from this section, I would quickly high light some observations made by business daily Economic Times (ET) on 22nd July, 2018. ET believes that Dubai is slowly but surely losing its appeal as a global business hub because there is a general feeling that Dubai's recipe for economic success is becoming stale. ET then states, why Dubai's dominance as a global travel hub is also on the wane. Growth in passenger numbers at Dubai International Airport is down to nearly zero after 15 years of impressive growth. This is mainly due to emergence of super, long range aircraft, with large numbers of non-stop flights directly connecting Asia to Europe and the Americas, thus bypassing Dubai.

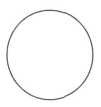

DUBAI'S AND INDIA'S CORRUPTION: THE LETHAL INTERNATIONAL COCKTAIL

Dubai has created a fantasyland with glamorous, world-class restaurants; the largest, highest man-made fountains; mind-boggling hotels; and stunning buildings. But what is the basis for and source of the funds for this growth? After all, there is no sustainable manufacturing base there; hardly any substantial, organized financial services sector, though they are trying to build one; and very limited oil and gas resources. Abu Dhabi, the UAE's capital, houses the majority of the country's oil and gas reserves. So, with a highly leveraged economy based on trade and mainly staffed by an expat community that pays no personal taxes, how is there any cash flow for Dubai itself?

According to figures provided by Dubai's government, the retail sector caters to a constantly changing population of about three million people, plus another fifteen million tourists who come to Dubai every year. In fact, tourism is one of the economy's mainstays, and many companies and industries are actively trying to boost tourism and make Dubai an airline hub. But even airlines are heavily subsidized by Abu Dhabi oil money and as mentioned in the previous chapter Dubai's dominance as a global travel hub is also on the wane.

So, to repeat the vital question: where does Dubai get its revenue? How does it sustain a high-cost infrastructure in an inhospitable desert climate?

In part, the money comes from investments from oil-rich places like Abu Dhabi, Saudi Arabia, Kuwait, and Qatar. Since these countries are all engaged in an economic pact, their nationals enjoy the same rights in Dubai as locals, so it is seen as an acceptable investment. In many ways, Dubai is like the Las Vegas of the Gulf—minus the casinos—and it provides excellent nightlife opportunities compared to places like Riyadh, Kuwait City, and Doha. The wealthy and even not-so-wealthy locals from these countries come to Dubai to play, so it makes sense for them to invest in this playground.

But that kind of investment is still not sufficient to fuel Dubai's tremendous growth. Dubai has created a great infrastructure, and it operates on the economic theory that supply may create its own demand. The famous saying, "If you build it, they will come," certainly rings true in Dubai. But who are the "they" that will come? Dubai's main trading partners: India, China, and Iran.

We do not have a great understanding of how China and Iran contribute to Dubai's growth, due to the secrecy both nations work under, though we do know they both have trading and manufacturing ties with Dubai. A lot of Iran's trade goes through Dubai, mostly when there is some kind of trade embargo or international sanctions against it. But India plays a much larger role in Dubai's continued sustenance than either country, and we will examine that in depth.

At this point, we need to take a step back and discuss India's primary woe—its endemic corruption—in more detail. India's GDP is now averaging an annual growth rate of 6 or 7 percent per year recently. This turn-around in the economy, which started in the early 1990s, has created a substantial middle class of about 250 million people. Yet despite the existence and increasing prominence of this affluent, well-educated, urban middle class, India still boasts over 330 million people—six times the population of the UK—without electricity in their homes. Most of these 330 million also do not even have a proper toilet, running water, or basic sanitation in their homes.

India's primary reaction to this poverty is to blame it on their nation's British-colonial past. The elite often simply shrug and say, "The British raped the country dry for over three hundred years, and we are still suffering from it." That may be partially true, but it does not justify a state of affairs in which, in this modern day, 330 million people must relieve themselves in the bushes every single day, a good seventy years after the British packed their bags and left India. Furthermore, if we look at Japan, another country that was occupied and whose infrastructure was largely destroyed by a Western power, we see a country that is now fully developed and, in fact, a world leader in technology. Japan makes India's excuses and blaming of the British look very frivolous indeed.

In reality, India has been plundered and destroyed by:

A   Corrupt politicians.

B   Corrupt bureaucrats, mainly from the excise, customs, income tax, and police departments.

C   The business community, which bribes their way through the tax offices, police, excise, licensing, and customs.

These three groups collaborate and co-operate extensively with each other at all levels of Indian society. In fact, it is almost impossible to name a single Indian government department that is free of corruption, whether at the state or federal level.

Merely looking at one category—India's bureaucrats—we can see that the level of corruption in India is on a truly epic scale. Are there any honest "government servants," as India's bureaucrats are known? There certainly must be, but they are few and far between.

To even become government servants, very hardworking, top-notch students with a great sense of national pride must compete for these positions by taking the Public Services Commission examination, which includes a gruelling written test and stringent interview process. This exam and the commission that runs it are a part of India's inheritance from the British Raj; the Indian Civil Service is an almost exact copy of the British Civil Service. Millions of Indian students take these examinations every year, and just a few thousand are selected for service across all the central government departments. Many take this exam again and again, year after year, hoping to secure prestigious government employment for life. Fortunately, there is no known corruption within the examinations and the selection process itself.

Delhi is the epicenter of this examination. The capital is dotted with specialist coaching centers aimed at helping young people ace these exams. Students from all over India who aspire to be India's newest government servants enrol in Delhi University under the pretense of pursuing postgraduate, doctoral, and post-doctoral degrees, when they are actually just in the city to take advantage of its coaching centres, and government subsidised student hostels to help them succeed in the gruelling exam. These individuals often pursue vague courses of study; for example, one might complete a master's degree in Sanskrit, a dead Indian language, and then immediately enroll in another master's program in Buddhist Studies, just to be able to pursue these exams year after year.

The top few hundred successful candidates are offered the most prestigious posts in the Indian Administrative Services (IAS). They are considered the country's future top mandarins. The next best of the crop are offered appointments in the Indian Foreign Services (IFS). They are the diplomatic corps, India's future ambassadors to places like London, Washington, D.C., and Paris. The remainder join departments such as Taxation Services, the police, or the Excise Department.

The two most popular postings for new government servants are the Foreign Services and the Taxation Services. The Foreign Services are popular because Indians love to live abroad and escape India. Some of the highest ranked young government servants willingly give up their first offer of a position in the IAS in favour of taking up a position in the diplomatic corps, which will give them the opportunity to travel the world and get away from the clutches of India's dishonest and corrupt politicians. On the other hand, the rush to join Taxation Services is based entirely on that branch's known corruption and the "opportunities" that come with such corruption.

After a year of academy-based training in their new program, the trainees return to the geographical bases of their choice to take up their official postings. It is here that we begin to see these young, hard-working, talented, and idealistic people have their moral compasses set askew.

The initial cause of this moral bankruptcy is peer pressure. It is the same kind of peer pressure that youngsters in the West face to dabble in alcohol and drug use. Faced with such pressure, it is almost impossible to survive as an honest government servant. If a young officer does not immediately join the established "bribery gravy train," they will be bullied both by their peers and their superiors. If that does not prove to be effective, they will be pushed away into "punishment postings."

An ex-colleague told me about a young officer in the state capital of Assam in north-eastern India who refused to toe the line and accept the expected bribes. Within six months of arriving, he was sent off to a punishment posting in a remote village in the state. Every morning, this young man now had to cross a small river on foot because there was neither any footbridge nor any public transportation. This commute to work wasn't too bad during the summer and winter months, when all he had to do was take off his shoes and roll up his trousers. But during the monsoon rains, the trek became hazardous in the extreme. The small stream would become a mad swirling river with huge undercurrents. There were days when the young man would make it to work, only to realize by early afternoon that the rains had triggered flash floods, and his only option was to stay in his small, cramped office for several days at a time. To make the daily trek even more exciting, he often came across a herd of wild elephants from the neighboring forest, calmly grazing while also keeping a suspicious eye out for any human mischief-makers in their territory.

This can be the penalty for non-compliance in such a corrupt state.

If idealism, patriotism, honesty, and integrity are so punished in India's elite government service, what should a young aspiring public servant in India do to cope? The recommended best practice is to simply shut your eyes (and your conscience) to rampant bribe-taking and corruption and join the gravy train as soon as possible. Especially in today's world of electronic and social media, if any such honest misfit, driven by values like integrity and honesty, does arrive in a traditionally corrupt department like police or taxation, the departmental strategy is to either get the newcomer to be compliant or get rid of him or her.

Just as resistance to the corrupt status quo is often harshly punished, compliance is very handsomely rewarded. For example, take the case of a young Income Tax officer in a suburban area of Calcutta who was very faithful to the existing system. He procured the expected bribes and passed on the exact designated amounts to his bosses, who in turn passed on the allocated shares to their bosses, thus ensuring that everyone in the food chain was taken care of. In doing so, the new recruit knew that he would be rewarded, and if he kept it up, he would eventually be taken out of the suburbs and posted to a proper business district where he could continue to assist businesses of all shapes and sizes avoid and evade taxes. This could result in significantly more bribes for him from such a thriving business area.

When the writer of this book visited a very educated and highly intelligent senior Income Tax officer at his residence in New Delhi, the author was extremely surprised to see hundreds of bags of rice stacked in the house, which was a residence in the very heart of the metropolis. Normally, the average middle-class person in urban India would have about half a bag of rice in the household at any given time. Therefore, seeing so many bags of rice was a slight anomaly.

On very innocently asking the Tax Officer friend why there were so many bags of rice in the house, this otherwise very communicative and gregarious person became shy, diffident, and sheepish. His wife came to his rescue when she very proudly explained that her husband's "customers," the firms from whom he was supposed to collect taxes, were some of the largest grocery traders in Delhi's Chandni Chowk area, and they would rather pay their bribes with bags of rice and flour than with cash. He, the tax man, the ever-accommodating, flexible, government servant, could hardly say no to such an offer, could he?

Tax evasion is practically a national pastime in India. Indian businessmen can come from any caste, creed, state, or industry, but the one common passion that binds them together is the question of how to minimize or avoid paying taxes altogether. Now, from the average Indian citizen's point of view, it is not difficult to understand why one would not want to pay taxes. They could easily think that they get little in return: India is plagued by dirty, filthy, dangerous roads; state medical care that is characterized by the lack of it; and even a lack of quality sanitation. But the businessman's attitude toward taxes is even more self-serving, and it comes down to, "This is my hard-earned money from my own enterprise. Why should I part with it?" This attitude is then given a boost from corrupt politicians and bureaucrats who take bribes at every stage to facilitate this unprecedented tax evasion.

Is there tax evasion in the UK, the United States, or other parts of the industrialized world? Of course there is. Do some Americans or Germans or Swedes resent having to pay taxes and refuse to pay their fair share? Of course they do. But that is nothing compared to the institutional approach that India and Indians have taken to tax evasion on an industrial scale.

In general, the funds that result from bribes and from tax evasion are known as "Black Money," and they are usually held either in cash in homes or in *benami* ("in other names") bank accounts, which exist in the names of one's spouse, children, children-in-law, or grandchildren. They are preferably kept in the name of very close family members, thanks to the guiding principle that blood is thicker than water. It is also sometimes invested in stocks, shares, and properties held by close family members. There is never any risk of that money being confiscated by the individual holding the property, as it is always done in absolute trust, and a deep social contract governs these types of holdings. The "Black Money" economy in India is almost as large as, if not larger than, the regular economy, and it is an important part of the nation's overall wealth.

The unholy alliance between the business community, government workers, and politicians that has given rise to the Black Money economy has set India back decades behind its closest economic competitor, China, and it has been devastating for the nation's social and economic growth. If we look at India's economic development from 1947—the year of its independence—to now, it is not difficult to understand why 330 million people still live below the poverty line, do not get even one full meal a day, do not have a proper roof over their heads, and do not have proper sanitation at home. Yet at the same time, another 250 million have a lifestyle that involves an entourage of servants, lavish weddings and funerals, and consumer goods the likes of which most people even in the West can only dream of. Clearly, part of the nation's population is experiencing a prosperity that is not reflected in the nation's overall economic growth.

If Japan, a nation that was heavily bombed and roundly defeated at the end of World War II, was able to regain its global economic powerhouse status less than twenty years after being nearly wiped from the face of the earth, then why does India, with its great educational infrastructure, spirit of enterprise, family values and work culture, still have a significant portion of its population submerged in grinding poverty nearly seventy years after independence from its colonial rulers? Why does the Indian elite abandon India to live abroad in English-speaking nations, in what is possibly the largest brain-drain in the annals of human civilization? The answers lie in India's corrupt nexus of politicians, business people, and the so-called "government servants" who have ruthlessly looted the country to the point of bankruptcy.

In fact, India has a population of 1.3 billion people, yet only 13 million—1 percent—pay any taxes at all. There is no reliable estimate for the total sum that is lost through tax evasion, though some estimate that the total amount of "Black Money" floating around India represents at least 23 percent of India's GDP, approximately US$1.3 trillion.

So why is all of this relevant to Dubai? It is simple: for a predatory economy like Dubai's, this "Black Money" is a huge resource in the immediate neighborhood, just waiting to be tapped.

Just how much of this "Black Money" makes its way into Dubai every year? No one really knows or even cares, though many suspect that much of it is funnelled in by way of property purchases. In fact, a significant number of new properties built in Dubai are quickly snapped up by entities in India, even though no Indians in their right minds who have lived in Dubai for any amount of time would ever make a long-term investment like property in Dubai if they value their hard-earned savings. Instead, those who have no intention to ever living in them are purchasing these buildings as investment properties.

So does the bulk of the money for property purchased in "no questions asked" Dubai come from laundered Indian funds or does it come from legitimate sources that have been officially cleared by the Reserve Bank of India? Like so many financial dealings in Dubai, no one really knows or even cares. So long as the checks clear , the money's legality doesn't enter into it.

Of course, the Indian old money, or *khandani amir*, as they are called in India, rarely use Dubai as an offshore base. They are mainly based in Mumbai, and due to Mumbai's proximity to Dubai, they have intimate knowledge of Dubai and, consequently, do not trust it. Instead, they have their complex webs of family-held trusts, private banking relationships with Swiss and other Western international bodies, and offshore companies, all held in places where they know and trust the rule of law, allowing them to manage their wealth securely with great peace of mind. These families have vast wealth, which they hand down from generation to generation, and they cannot and will not take any chances with it in a place like Dubai. To put it simply: they park their yachts safely in Monaco Harbour, not the more dubious Dubai Marina.

Thus, it is the Indian nouveau riche, who use *hawala*, the indigenous, unregulated peer-to-peer money transfer system, which we will cover in more detail in the next section, to get their "Black Money" out of India and into Dubai,India's nearest Panama City.

Recently, the Indian government under Narendra Modi began a dramatic campaign to get "Black Money" out of circulation. Since so much "Black Money" changes hands in the form of 500 and 1000 Indian Rupee notes, they are demonetizing these notes, a near-Herculean task. This is not a new idea, and many leaders going as far back as the 1970s have tried to or threatened to make efforts to cull the illicit stockpile of laundered funds. Modi is just the first one brave enough to actually make a stand of this nature.

How effective this will actually be is anyone's guess. It's possible that the rich and famous were tipped off before the launch of this campaign and already made efforts to invest all of their "Black Money" funds abroad. All we do know is that as a result of this policy, the poorest experienced severe economic distress, while the rich and super-rich snapped up billions of dollars of alternative assets, such as gold and Rolex watches, before this new policy kicked in. Still, Modi's efforts should be lauded, because at least he understands the nature of India's true malaise and is trying to cull what is possibly the worst corruption in the world.

We are already seeing the results of this crackdown. In late 2016, when exhibitors from Dubai hosted the annual property showcase in Mumbai, they experienced quite a shock when very few prospective buyers showed up. With so much of the Indian "Black Money" becoming useless, its holders cannot transfer it out of India to make such purchases in Dubai.

In fact, outside of India itself, Dubai is the place that has most felt the impact of India's demonetization of its high-value notes. Around the time that this policy went into effect, a low-profile, but still powerful, Dubai team that oversaw construction projects in the emirate shut down several departments, with the loss of a large number of expatriate jobs. Seventeen senior locals lost their jobs as well, which is quite unprecedented. Due to the opaque nature of business in Dubai, it is unknown whether these closures were due to the curtailing of "Black Money" in India or the sharp fall in oil prices around that time.

So does India's extreme corruption and the billions of dollars of illicit "Black Money" that this corruption generates actively contribute to Dubai's existence, survival, and most importantly, its growth and international recognition? Does it affect Dubai more than fluctuating oil prices? Consider that prior to the discovery of oil in the region, Dubai was nothing more than a small fishing village. It survived and grew in those early years by smuggling gold into India. As far as Dubai was concerned, this was just a part of a free-trade economy and what India or any other country might view as smuggling, they are simply viewed as re-exporting.

As a result, literally tons of gold were ferried across the Arabian Sea in local boats, known as *dhows*, and dumped along India's vast western coastline at a time when gold imports into India were strictly banned. This gold re-export operation was done in close collaboration with the corrupt Indian police, the Coast Guard, politicians, and another very prominent industry in India: the criminal underworld. What this did to the Indian economy was none of Dubai's concern; as long as the *dhows* continued to go back and forth between India's western coast and Dubai and there was money to be made in the process, it made complete sense for Dubai to continue doing so.

Many in Dubai firmly believe that the emirate's current local business elite began their journey to prosperity by smuggling gold into India in the 1960s and 1970s and that the money made from that operation, which was legitimate on the Dubai end, was further legitimized by circulating it in Dubai legally. More appropriately, to use the jargon of money laundering, the money from the gold operation was nicely "layered" and "integrated" into Dubai's mainstream economy by investments in properties and hotels and acquiring dealerships and franchises of premium car brands, luxury goods, and electronic goods, which had a surge in domestic demand in the early 1970s, due to the regional boom created by the discovery of oil. The oil boom in and around Dubai gave locals the disposable income to indulge in conspicuous consumption, which then firmly established and legitimised the funds generated from Dubai's export and re-export economy.

Thus, with its crude—yet highly successful—Indian gold operation, the Dubai Leadership Team recognized and understood that there was money to be made in imports and re-exports, depending on the shortage of a particular commodity somewhere in the region. They shrewdly capitalized on this idea and built up Dubai into a major entrepôt. The great Jebel Ali Port, which, if local gossip is to be believed, can be seen from the moon, was born from this very idea.

Thus, Dubai is trying to become a multicultural melting pot and all-inclusive society where professionals from Wall Street, powerful exiled politicians, generals toppled by coups, petty thugs, evil gangsters, up-and-coming businessmen, and ordinary people live happily side-by-side, so long as they have no returned checks, no fistfights, no shouting matches, and they bow in deference to the locals.

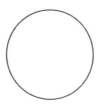

HAWALA: INFORMAL MONEY TRANSFERS

Slowly but surely, Dubai is ridding itself of its "small fishing village and smugglers' cove" image as it reinvents itself as a regional financial powerhouse capable of competing with, and possibly someday surpassing, its main rivals, Singapore and Hong Kong. The emirate's leaders want to establish Dubai as the financial capital of Asia, a strategically positioned gateway connecting the East and West. To internationalize and modernize Dubai's image, it has established stock and commodity exchanges similar to those found in London, New York, and Tokyo, monitored by financial professionals from the Western world and highly skilled subject matter experts from the rest of the world. It is a grand, audacious plan that thus far seems to be paying off.

But even as Dubai reaches for the stars and tries to compete with London and New York in the official markets, should it also congratulate itself on another status it has reportedly achieved ? This achievement, which cannot be officially confirmed due to its very nature, is of being a hotbed for—indeed, reportedly the international capital of—informal banking (nicknamed the 'Dubai Laundromat' by those who are familiar with its operations) and *hawala* operations. *Hawala* is a term that Asians, especially Indians and other citizens of the subcontinent, are very familiar with, but it is often a new concept to Western audiences.

Hawala is the unorganized, below-the-radar, non-regulated foreign exchange market, which offers significantly better conversion rates and is commission-free, super-fast, totally confidential, untraceable, paperless, and queue-free. It offers the ability to move money without any electronic or auditable trail.

They say that imitation is the best compliment, and the West has recently imported this business model, calling it "peer-to-peer" (P2P)-funded money transfers, in which money is transferred without assets physically crossing jurisdictions, a system very similar to that of *hawala*. But P2P transfer firms have a formal structure and are somewhat loosely regulated. It will take the West's P2P system several decades to match *hawala*'s discretion, service, and only-can-be-dreamt-of exchange rates, which are at least 10- to 15-percent better than the official FX markets on any given day.

Wikileaks has provided extensive details on how the Middle

Eastern elite uses this free movement of funds to pursue their own agendas, which is beyond the scope of this book. Our focus here is on the operational flexibility of *hawala* and how easily, effortlessly, and seamlessly it works and thrives in Dubai.

This is how *hawala* transactions work. Let us say an Indian man based in Dubai—though similar transactions can be undertaken for anyone anywhere in the world—wants to send Rs 100,000 to India for personal reasons, such as a sister's marriage, building a house, his parents' medical care, or his son's college education. Now, if he went to the bank or an official exchange firm, which are plentiful in Dubai, he would get an official exchange rate of, say, US$1=Rs 65. (All currencies in the Gulf are tied to the US dollar. The UAE Dirham has a fixed conversion rate of US$1=Dhs 3.673.) He would then pay a commission fee and fill out paperwork that would inevitably create an audit trail.

If, instead, he used the *hawala* route, he would get an exchange rate at least 10- to 15-percent better than what he would get on the official market. So, for every US dollar-equivalent-dirham, he would get about twelve or thirteen more rupees than the official rate would give him. Even more importantly though, there is no paperwork and no commission fee. No questions are asked about the source of the funds on the Dubai side or their ultimate destination and purpose in India. Additionally, the transfer of funds is extremely rapid. If a licensed exchange house were to deliver the funds the next day, which is the earliest possible delivery, they would charge a few extra dollars as a "rush fee." There is no such thing with *hawala*, making it both speedy and very cost-effective. Please also note that Dubai pursues a free exchange policy and since there is no personal taxation yet, there is nothing illegal about this process on the Dubai end.

In order to make use of this system, all you need to do is know someone who knows someone else who is a *hawala* operator. It could be a small shop owner, a sales executive in a local firm, or just any individual who has become an agent to support his or her income, similar to how people become part-time Uber drivers or freelance Amazon couriers in the West. The people who run these sorts of operations are often regular "guys next door."

Once you have this connection, all you have to do is approach the *hawala* agent and say you want to send some funds abroad. Often, the agent will initially give you a blank look, as if he or she doesn't understand what you are saying. At that point, you simply need to drop the name of the person who sent you to the agent in a slightly confidential manner: "I am Bobby's friend," or, "Sultan sent me." That's all you need. At that, the *hawala* operator will ask for the cash, count it, and confirm where you want it sent. He or she will then give the day's rate for that city.

At that point, the operator will put the cash in a safe and provide you with a telephone number in the exact overseas city where you want the money sent, in all probability a pay-as-you-go mobile number. He or she will give you instructions to call that number and say, "So-and-so in such-and-such city asked me to call you," and let them know the precise amount of money that will be available in its destination city. After that, you just need to tell the money's intended recipient, "Please call so-and-so at this phone number to pick up this amount of cash." That's it.

The transaction reportedly happens very rapidly. For example, if someone arranges to send money from Dubai to Mumbai around 11 a.m., it will be available to the beneficiary in India by late afternoon. It is ruthlessly efficient and completely based on personal trust. No one knows how the *hawala* markets are determined or how the exchange rate is set for the day. Some say it is directly correlated with the price of gold, but that is purely speculation—just like everything else in this business.

Apart from excellent service, the utmost discretion, and phenomenally good rates, *hawala* transactions flow across all borders and cut through all exchange-control regulations, which are still in place for countries like India. Even today, outward remittances beyond a certain threshold require formal permission from the Reserve Bank of India. But with outbound *hawala* transactions, this can easily be circumvented.

Given this system's clear superiority, why hasn't *hawala* become more mainstream? For one thing, *hawala* is not run by members of mainstream society, especially in places like India. The Indian nouveau riche are often targeted for robbery, blackmail, and kidnapping by criminal groups immediately after making outbound money transfers through *hawala*.

It is common for unscrupulous *hawala* operators to come to the customer's residence to pick up the cash, so that the nouveau riche will not be seen seeking out a *hawala* office. After they get the cash, the agent then informs their criminal colleagues of where they can find this residence and how much "Black Money" they may have there. These criminals can then rob the home at their leisure; after all, the victim can hardly call the police to report a robbery of their own illicit funds. This would eventually lead to having to bribe the investigating police officers just to hush up the existence of "Black Money" on the property. It's all more trouble than it's worth.

Of course, the West and the rest of the world talks about and condemns things like money laundering, illicit fund transfers, and *hawala*, yet they are perfectly aware of and look the other way when it comes to these sorts of operations in Dubai and the UAE.[16] After all, if they were to expose the truths about these sheikhdoms, who would buy their weapons, their military aircraft, their private jets and yachts, their luxury cars, and their newest technologies, such as the Hyperloop? Keep in mind that the United States recently sold $100 million-worth of arms to one of the most repressive states in the world, Saudi Arabia. In the commercial Air Shows organised by Dubai all major aircraft manufacturers like Boeing, Airbus and Gulfstream etc, assemble to exhibit and sell their latest products, billions of dollars change hands. In the face of such huge sums of money, no one really cares about the small transactions that *hawala* enables, though everyone is fully aware of the devastating

---

16. You can read more about why Dubai and the UAE is such an attractive place for such international operations to flourish, thanks to its unregulated banking sector: https://uk.finance.yahoo.com/news/top-10-countries-where-british-112814168.html.

consequences to the general public that can come about due to such unfettered, worldwide money transfers.

In the meantime, the message for the Indian nouveau rich is: you can use the *hawala* system to save a few hundred dollars on exchange rates, but you will also run the risk of losing a couple million through a home robbery. Everything has a price in the end. This writer's advice is to pay a little extra for an official exchange rate and sleep well at night. After all, you get what you pay for in life. The international community should make careful note of this particular aspect of Dubai's economy.[17]

---

17. If you want to know more about Dubai's banking system, you can read more here: https://economictimes.indiatimes.com/industry/banking/finance/banking/25-countries-in-global-banks-high-risk-list/articleshow/64863022.cms?utm_source=ETnotifications&utm_medium=autopush&utm_campaign=Banking&utm_content=10AM.

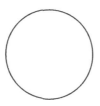

DUBAI AND PROFESSIONALISM

Gleaming hotels; clean, modern highways good enough for an aircraft landing; mind-boggling high-rises from whose windows Russian models hang without safety nets for selfies to post on Instagram and Facebook; celebrity endorsements from A-listers in Bollywood and Hollywood; mega-malls. Dubai must be the most professional place on earth; otherwise, how could such magical things exist there?

In reality, Dubai exists—and even thrives—with a serious case of "conflict of interest." The whole of the UAE actively encourages its own citizens to make money "on the side" and top-up their government-job salaries, which are already disproportionately high by any standards. After they wrap up their eight a.m.-to-two p.m. jobs in the banks, the Immigration Department, or the police, locals step out in droves with a Dubai-style entrepreneurial spirit to run their own businesses or sponsor other foreign businesses, for which they get a cushy annual sponsorship fee. It does not matter what or who they sponsor so long as the foreigner can cough up the requisite cash. Thus, Dubai is practically the embodiment of "conflict of interest" at its best—or worst. On the other hand, it is also considered the epitome of free enterprise, and the view a person takes on this matter is totally dependent on their particular circumstances and experiences.

Take the case of Ibrahim Anwar, an acquaintance of this author and a local of non-local descent. He is a UAE citizen and is always attired in the local dress, yet his father originally came to Dubai many years ago from a neighbouring country when Dubai was just a sleepy fishing village. He became a naturalized UAE citizen, thus allowing his family to inherit the UAE nationality.

After completing his education in Dubai, Ibrahim Anwar went to the American University of Beirut just before the Lebanese Civil War broke out. Anwar then returned to Dubai, joined the Bank Universal (not the real name), and quickly rose through the ranks to become one of the youngest local branch managers in that bank.

In general, locals have far superior career paths in any organization compared to their expatriate peers. In fact, the entire idea of having a "career path" in any organization, whether it be the government, banks, or oil firms, is entirely reserved for locals. Foreigners are regarded as temporary workers, so they do not need a "career path" in Dubai though they could be around in any organisation for decades, if needed by Dubai.

Thus, locals are fast-tracked to promotions, even if they lack the requisite skills. Locals also have a different—and better—salary structure than expatriates, and they are all entitled to a "local allowance" from the Government, over and above their salaries. All of this is part of a cynical yet practical ploy on the part of the Dubai government to ensure that their citizens are kept happy, thinking only about their next holiday or their next car and not about things like free speech and Arab Spring-style uprisings.

Despite his excellent salary with the bank, Anwar, like most other locals, worked "full-time" at the bank (full-time being from eight a.m. to two p.m.) and also started a general trading firm, Euro-Japan Trading, on the side after working hours. He also sponsored multiple expat businesses and even a "shady" money transfer firm which was reportedly involved in *hawala* transactions. Through his general trading firm, Anwar bought white goods, such as refrigerators, washing machines, stoves, and dishwashers, from various destinations in Southeast Asia and distributed them through local shops in Dubai or re-exported them to Iran or Yemen.

Fluent in Hindi, Urdu, Gujarati, Arabic, and Iranian (also known as Farsi), Anwar had fledgling Dubai at his feet. Big Indian and Asian traders in Dubai trusted him blindly because they identified with him through his roots. He, in turn, held an influential position in a local bank as a *kandura*-wearing local, and he could secure funding for their trading activities whenever they wanted. It was a very cozy relationship all round.

Commercial banking facilities in Dubai are very basic, mostly dealing with two different kinds of Letters of Credit

(L/c's): Documents against Payments (DP) and Documents against Acceptance (DA). To fund the L/c's, there is a facility called a Trust Receipt (TR), where traders can release the documents and, hence, the goods imported under that L/c. Settlement periods vary from bank to bank and from customer to customer, so to secure bank facilities, it is quite helpful if the foreigner knows someone who knows someone else who knows the credit approving banker.

As we've mentioned before, Dubai is an entrepôt, and the bulk of its business is import and re-export. This business model has paper-thin margins, and the secret of success in it lies in the trader's ability to buy low and sell high, just like with any other trading operation anywhere else in the world and to a known customer group.

For example, a Dubai-based trader in white goods will first locate a manufacturer or a franchisee of a household brand in Taiwan or Malaysia who can supply him with a branded item, such as a washing machine, for just one dollar per piece less than the going market rate. Then, the trader can make one hundred thousand dollars simply by importing several shipping containers of these washing machines into Dubai, changing the shipping documents so that the buyer does not know the supplier details, and then re-export the containers to the Iranian port city of Bander Abbas by boat or perhaps to Saudi Arabia or Oman by road. The most crucial part of the entire transaction is in knowing the exact details of the supplier and the terms by which they are willing to do business.

Nearly all such transactions are done by supplying the

overseas supplier with a letter of credit from one of the reputable banks in Dubai. One of the major privileges and tasks of a local branch manager—such as Anwar—is the authority to approve and sign off on every single letter of credit application that is submitted by the trading firms in Dubai that have a business relationship with the bank. Thus, Anwar was fully in a position to use—or rather, misuse—the trust that was placed in him by his employers and the bank's clients.

Each day, he would hold all the letter of credit applications that were given to him to sign off on during banking hours under the pretext of scrutinizing them further to ensure that they would not pose any risk to the bank. In reality, after the staff had gone home at two p.m., he would quietly sit alone in his office and copy down all of the confidential information from the applications: the supplier's name, the goods being shipped, the purchase price, and the contract terms—in short, the client's vital, confidential business information on which their very livelihood depended. After copying down all of this information, Anwar would go home to his own trading company business and then negotiate a similar or even better deals for his operation with his client's suppliers.

Anywhere else in the world, this would be considered downright unprofessional at best and a serious conflict of interest, a breach of trust and data protection, or even outright fraud at worst. But not so in Dubai; there, such doings are the norm and are not seen as a problem. In fact, Anwar's local colleagues in other bank branches did the same thing.

Herein lies the different style of corruption in the UAE

compared to that of other emerging economies like India's. The corrupt Indian government tax official knows he is doing something wrong and is always on the defensive and watching his back as a result. His children know that the standard of living they enjoy is disproportionate to their father's official income and are very nervous whenever his job status comes up for discussion among their friends.

But in the UAE, this is an accepted part of life. A local banker would not consider it untoward to sponsor an expatriate business, use his power and position to grant that same business millions of dollars of credit from his own bank, and also steal that business's confidential deal-making edge. The idea of "conflict of interest" does not even exist in Dubai. There is no such thing as corruption; it is simply the locals' birth right to pocket as much cash as they can, regardless of the source of these funds.

Anwar's business practice is Dubai's most sustainable business model. He has an assured regular cash flow from his day job's salary, and he also uses the privileges of that role to enrich his private side enterprise. Conflict of interest? What conflict of interest? Client data protection? What client data protection? As long as there is cash to be made, nothing else matters in Dubai. *Khalli walli* data protection.

But there was much more to it than that. Anwar also employed his brother-in-law, Vaashin, as both the bank branch's marketing assistant and his own business's marketing assistant—and with both roles on the bank's payroll. Vaashin's job was to go to small expat businesses in the Pur Dubai area every evening and introduce himself as the local bank branch manager's brother-in-law. He would inform them that he had enough influence with his brother-in-law to provide them with banking facilities, thus drumming up new business. Once these local business owners acquired access to the bank's facilities, they would generally open letters of credit, thus giving Anwar access to even more information about supplier sources.

Vaashin may or may not have asked for bribes upfront from the businesses he introduced to the bank, but once they had accounts there, he would go back to these businesses and ask for favours from the owners: "A friend of mine has passed away, and his widow cannot afford to get the body home. Could you please assist with the funeral expenses?" or "My sister's son needs an operation. Could you please help us pay for it?" And, of course, the business owners would be obliged to cough up some money for the local bank branch manager's brother-in-law who had helped them. It was a simple, but effective, scam.

In another recent case, an Indian banker in Dubai and his assistant sold complex derivative-based products, as a capital-guaranteed investment product to a Gulf national and his elderly mother. When the credit crunch came to Dubai in 2008, the position unraveled, and the family lost nearly one hundred million dollars.

The case went to the DIFC court, and the judge questioned the banker about the complex product and his own understanding of the mathematical model on which the product was based. The professional banker replied that the last time he had done any math was while he was in school. Here was an investment banker who had sold a complex, multi-million-dollar derivative product to a pair of unsophisticated investors yet had no understanding of the most basic algebraic equations required to analyze the risk-return attributes of the product and the risk tolerance profile of a potential investor.These calculations and adherence to due diligence processes are mandatory prior to any suitable investment recommendations made by a competent investment adviser. However in Dubai ,it appears,that there is no need to adhere to any such 'best practice' in client care.

In this case though, the judge ruled in favor of the local family and declared it the worst case of misleading financial promotion he had ever witnessed. He found the defendant to be in gross breach of professional standards and having profoundly benefitted personally by misleading unsuspecting and unsophisticated clients.[18]

However, despite the judge's ruling, this individual continues to operate in the Dubai International Financial Centre (DIFC) as an investment adviser with permission to advise retail clients. This is professionalism, Dubai-style.

18. You can read more about it Dubai International Financial Centre case number CFI 026/2009, Rafed al Khorafi v Bank Sarasin.

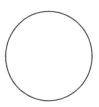

THE MISERY OF INDIA'S POOREST AND DUBAI'S SKYSCRAPERS

We have already discussed how India's rampant corruption and "Black Money" could possibly feed, support, and perpetuate Dubai's economy. These funds come from India's upper- and burgeoning middle classes looking for an outlet for their unpaid income taxes and illicit hoarded wealth.

But not only has Dubai been metaphorically and financially built by India, serving as its very own backyard Panama City with no fear of the leaked Panama Papers,[19] it was also literally built by India's poorest, who were simply trying to make a better life for themselves than what they could secure back

19. You can read more about the Panama Papers here: www.icij.org/investigations/panama-papers/.

home. In fact, the poorest of the poor come from all across the developing world—India, Pakistan, Nepal, Bangladesh, Sri Lanka, Phillipines etc.—to build Dubai's skyscrapers.

In many ways, these individuals are slave labor, with no rights of any kind. They must live where they are told to live—which is often labor camps—and work where and when they are told to work—which is often outside during the hottest part of the day. They are generally construction workers who must labor for hours on end in temperatures of 51 degrees centigrade (124 degrees Fahrenheit) or higher. Many return to their respective home countries in coffins. This is true not only of Dubai, but of the entire Gulf region. Qatar is using an identical labour system to build its 2022 World Cup football stadiums. The human rights issues surrounding these labour practices have received increasing international scrutiny in recent years.

Many of these labourers' stories are very much the same: they frequently come from the rural areas of developing nations, have little formal education, and are helping to support large, multi-generational families. They see coming to Dubai or Qatar or Saudi Arabia as the chance of a lifetime, an opportunity to help pull their family out of generations of abject poverty. Unfortunately, due to this background, they are easily tricked by unscrupulous "employment agents" who charge them exorbitant fees for the "privilege" of working in Dubai. Thus, they and their families often must go into a great deal of debt just to get them there.

When I lived in Dubai, I knew one such young man engaged in menial labour. His name was Ram, and his was a farming family that was just barely eking out an existence in the central Indian state of Madhya Pradesh. He had quit school after his *Madhyamik*, or year 10, due to a combination of lack of finances to continue and lack of academic prowess to successfully compete in India's highly competitive education system. By his early twenties, Ram was supporting a wife and child, along with his aging father who could no longer get up with the sunrise and work all day; an ailing mother who constantly complained of severe body aches and lived fifty miles from any kind of medical care; and two unmarried sisters, both of whom had left school at the age of twelve and whom Ram was now duty-bound to marry off. This whole family was dependent on a monthly income of Rs 5,000 in a good month—this translates to six adults and a child surviving on only US$75 per month. At that level, the family could barely afford one square meal per day. Making matters worse, the baby was already showing signs of serious malnutrition and needed vitamins, which were quite costly.

It was against this background that Ram heard about an employment agent from Mumbai with lucrative job offers from the Arabian Gulf city of Dubai. Ram was familiar with Dubai: he had seen the city on TV during cricket matches and was impressed with its beautiful tall buildings. Ram had also heard that Dubai was a very rich place and that anyone who was lucky enough to go there became rich beyond their wildest imagination; the streets were paved with gold, and salaries were in a currency tied to the American dollar. Ram decided to see if he could secure a job for himself in Dubai. He believed he had nothing to lose and everything to gain.

Ram eventually secured a job as a construction laborer for one of the biggest Arab firms. What Ram did not know was that outside temperatures in Dubai often reach 53 Degrees Centigrade (about 127 degreed Fahrenheit). He was promised a salary of US$300 per month—a sum he and his family had never even dreamed of—all tax-free, plus accommodations and the airline tickets to Dubai. This newfound wealth would attract many prospective bridegrooms for his sisters and would enable the family to purchase vitamins for his child, medicine for his aging parents, and new saris and jewelry for his wife. Maybe they could even afford to install a toilet in the house! The possibilities seemed endless.

Of course, whenever something sounds too good to be true, it often is. Everything in life comes with a price. In this case, the price was an advance payment of one hundred thousand rupees, around US$1400, which had to be paid upfront, to cover the cost of his tickets, visas, employment agent's fees, and other necessary paperwork. This was an astronomical sum of money for this family, and they had no idea how they would get their hands on such a huge payout.

The mother parted with her entire life savings, as well as the only two remaining gold bangles she had received from her parents when she got married. The two sisters pawned their only gold earrings, and the wife pawned her only jewellery: her wedding necklace. The father even sold the ring his grandfather had given him as a child. In addition, the family pawned the very land they owned, as well as their two cows and three goats.

They were prepared to give up everything to get Ram to Dubai so that he could change all of their fortunes.

After a two-day train journey to Mumbai, Ram was rushed from the train station to the Mumbai airport. He had never been in such a large city before, and he was overwhelmed by everything: the tall buildings, the hustle and bustle everywhere, and all the people. At the station, he joined a group of at least fifteen other men like him from all over India, all bound for Dubai and the same construction company. They were all excitedly looking forward to making some cash in Dubai to send back home to their families in India, just like him.

On the ride from the train station to the airport, their handlers instructed these men on what to do when they got to the airport, what happens at passport control, what questions the immigration officers would ask, etc. They cautioned the men that the airlines would serve alcohol with the food during their flight, but they strongly advised them not to drink too much or even skip it altogether, because Dubai is very strict about punishing drunkenness.

At the airport, the men stuck together in a herd. Once they had all gotten through passport control, they walked through a glass tunnel together, and Ram was awestruck by the sound and speed of the incoming and outgoing aircraft. He pinched himself, just to remind himself that this was happening to him. He had never even seen an aircraft up close before, and all of a sudden, in the course of few life-changing days, he had traveled to Mumbai and was now about to board his very first flight, which would cross at least one ocean.

When group finally boarded their aircraft, they were herded straight to the back. Ram had never seen anything like this before: to him, the inside of the aircraft looked like a king's palace in Bollywood movies. There were bright lights, music, and even a small television attached to the back of the seat in front of him. He had never sat in such a comfortable chair ever before.

The aircraft's take-off was a bit scary. There was a great deal of noise, and the speed made Ram's head spin. His ears became blocked, and he could not hear anything. He was frozen in his seat, simply too stunned by the plush luxury of his fairy tale surroundings and the strange sensations of the flight.

Soon enough, as the agent had promised in Mumbai, the crew began serving hot food with *daru* (alcohol). Ram was too scared to try any alcohol, but he was also rather uneasy about the food. The crew served it with spoons, special plates, and other items Ram wasn't sure how to use and when. Somehow, he and his colleagues managed to clean up the delicious hot food by copying what the other passengers were doing.

When the flight finally touched down in Dubai, Ram and his colleagues exited the aircraft through the gate bridge directly into the airport. They were startled by how cold it was. Ram wondered, *Why do they call Dubai hot? I am nearly freezing!* Of course, he was not aware that the icy blasts of air were coming straight from the airport's central air-conditioning unit. Soon enough, he would learn about Dubai's summer temperatures.

Despite the cold, he was awestruck by the airport's beauty; he had never seen anything so shiny and beautiful in his life.

He was so engrossed in admiring the lovely chandeliers and the marble floors that were squeaky-clean to the point of being slippery that he did not realize that he had arrived at the front of the immigration desk queue.

When Ram gave his passport to the officer sitting behind the desk, he did not realize that, in his mental preoccupation with his beautiful surroundings, he had forgotten to fill out a particular form. He now recalled that the agent had said something about a form that all Indians had to fill out when they arrived, but it was too late: the young officer was very angry and rude, waving Ram's passport in his face and saying something in a mixture of Arabic and Urdu.

Ram understood that he had to go to the back of the queue and fill out the necessary form, but he did not know what form it was or where to find it. The same thing happened to everyone in his group, and they all trooped to the back of the line, scared and nervous. They huddled together, not sure what to do next. Fortunately, one of them had figured out which particular form they had not filled out and found it at an empty desk in the arrivals hall. They all helped each other fill it out, and then quietly trooped back to the immigration desk's long queue.

This time, Ram encountered a different young local officer that was even ruder than the last. He stamped Ram's passport with great force and said, "*Yallah jaldi* [get going quickly]." Ram didn't have to be told twice. He scampered out of the immigration area and joined his colleagues, who were now huddled together near the baggage claim.

Suddenly a big, burly, bearded man approached the group

and asked in pidgin Hindi, "Have you come from India to work for Sheikh Sahib Company (not the real name)?" The men all nodded vigorously, having recognized the name of their new employer. They were quite relieved that someone had come to receive them in this strange foreign land.

The bearded gentleman then waved the group toward some men and women wearing a green uniform: the airport police. Ram and his colleagues panicked for a few moments, wondering what they had done wrong now. It turns out that all of their belongings had to go through the airport's x-ray scanner, which none of them had known about. Once each man's suitcase came out of the machine at the other end, they were escorted to a corner individually and asked to open their suitcases. The airport police then made a thorough search of everything in their very frugal luggage.

Even after this intrusive search, the policemen were very rude to the men; they were infuriated that they had not found anything incriminating in their meager possessions. Ram overheard the policemen commenting on the group, saying, "*Kachra Hindi* [dirty Indians]," again and again.

The men hastily packed up their belongings and returned to their corner. Once they had all regrouped, their employer's bearded agent re-joined them and simply said, "All of you, hand over your passports to me." The men were a bit baffled and frightened by this request; they had not heard anything about handing over their passports. They looked at each other, but no one put up even the slightest resistance or asked why they had to hand over their passports to a complete stranger. The agent in India had told them that if they expressed even the slightest displeasure or annoyance at anything, they would be on their way back to their villages in India very quickly. Thus, they were quick to comply with such a request.

What Ram and his friends did not know was that this request is the basis of Dubai's—and the Gulf's—infamous *kafala* system, a kind of twenty-first-century slavery. Under this system, all employers hold their employees' passports, essentially holding them prisoner.

Despite this, it was not until they stepped out of the airport into the Dubai evening that Ram had his first serious doubts about his entire journey to Dubai. It was around 8:30 p.m. in May, and while he had been repeatedly told that Dubai is hot, he was not prepared for just how hot it actually was. As the group exited the airport's centrally air-conditioned lobby, they were hit by a blast of hot air the likes of which they had never experienced even in the hottest months in India. Within seconds, they were all completely drenched in sweat.

The men trooped after their minder in a single-file line. As they crossed the road, they were impressed by the beautiful, fast cars driven by locals that screeched past them, not even willing to stop for pedestrians at designated crossings. They passed many other beautiful cars near the airport, some of which were gathering dust,and Ram wondered how rich the country must be to let such costly cars collect dust near the airport!

The men were expecting a minivan of sorts, but instead, they found that their minder had come to pick them up in a huge, open-top truck with two rows of seats in the back. They clambered onto the truck with their frugal belongings, and Ram found himself wondering what it would be like to travel in these open-top trucks through the rage of the mid-afternoon desert sun and heat. All of these negative thoughts fled though as their truck made its way through clean, wide, paved roads. There were not even roads like these in the bigger Indian cities like Mumbai, New Delhi, and Bangalore.

They soon came to a large open area filled with many caravan-like structures; the driver informed them that they had arrived at their new home: the famous—or infamous—Sonarpur Labour Camp of Dubai. Most construction businesses house their laborers in places like this, but Sonarpur is the largest and most well-known of such camps.

The group's initial reactions were quite positive. For one thing, the name "Sonarpur" has very positive connotations in India. "*Sona*" means "gold," and "*pur*" means "a place where people live." Thus, put together, it means "Golden City." What better place for these men from India to start their new lives in Dubai? In addition, the men were quite impressed with the accommodations provided. The caravans looked far more comfortable and luxurious than the thatched-roofed cottages back home. Little did these men know that Sonarpur also houses the only electric crematorium in Dubai.

The men settled into their new homes and bunk beds, very much aware that they had an early morning the next day. But as the night wore on, the sweltering heat kept most of the newcomers awake. Most of the accommodations only had fans; very few had air conditioners. The newcomers kept thinking of the cool breezes that came through after sunset even on the hottest of days back home.

As promised, the truck driver returned early the next morning and herded all of the newcomers back into his truck. But rather than going to a work site, they headed to Sheikh Rashid General Hospital. Ram had always enjoyed very good health and could not understand the need to go to a hospital before starting a new job. When they got off the truck in the hospital parking lot, the driver explained that they were all required to have a blood test to make sure they weren't carrying any communicable diseases, like TB, which is common in developing countries like India, and, more importantly, AIDS. Ram heaved a sigh of relief, because as far as he knew, he had neither.

After an hour of waiting, Ram's name was called, and he rushed into the testing area and submitted his blood. After waiting for the technician to process his results, he was directed out, and the truck driver met him and pointed him back to the truck. Ram was apparently the last one they were waiting for, because the vehicle was ready to move out, but he immediately noticed that there were now fewer men aboard it.

Ram had struck up a friendship with Mustafa, a young man about his own age from the Indian state of Kerala, who possessed considerably more knowledge about Dubai and the Gulf than all of them put together. Mustafa had said that almost every single household in his village had at least one person either in Dubai or somewhere else in the Gulf.

When Ram asked where the other missing men in his group

were, Mustafa lowered his voice and explained in a hushed tone that the missing men had failed the blood test. The police were detaining them in the hospital, and they would be taken to a special immigration detention unit at the airport until their sponsor arrived with their passport and a return ticket. They would then be sent back to India on the next available flight.

Ram wondered how these men would now pay off the debts they had incurred to come to Dubai in the first place.

Once the blood tests were over, Ram and his colleagues were sent over to another queue, where they were asked to peer into a dark black box so that the police could collect the details of their eyes. Ram became very frightened at this point and started wondering, *Why are they scanning my eyes? Am I going to be deported for some reason?* This was all very strange to Ram, but he kept quiet, thinking of his family, who were relying on him.

After completing this round of formalities, the men re-boarded the truck. The mid-day desert sun was now beating down viciously, and the men all put some kind of protection over their heads to ward off the scorching rays.

Ram noticed that there were now even fewer men in the truck than before, and Mustafa explained that there was some kind of problem with the new missing faces. They, too, would be sent home and were now being detained at the police station until immigration officially could collect them and deport them.

At this rate, Ram thought, *how many of us will be left at the end of the first day?* He was scared, but also seething with anger about the way his employment broker had presented the whole scenario in Dubai. He had never mentioned anything about trips to hospitals or police stations. In India, things like fingerprinting and eye scans are meant for criminals, not for normal people looking for work.

When they arrived back at the labor camp in the early evening, Ram was on the verge of swooning from the intense heat and the lack of food all day. Hungry, tired, and unbearably hot, all of the survivors of this Dubai version of *The X-Factor* Match Day 1 were then handed a bunch of papers to sign, all of which were written in Arabic. The men did not know whether they were signing their lives away or were joining the film crew of the latest Bollywood blockbuster.

Some of the older workers offered Ram and Mustafa some food from their own meager plates. Later, as they climbed into their bunk beds, Ram heard horror stories from the veteran workers about how salaries could be delayed for months at a time and how workers could be sent back to their home countries without any notice. No one ever knew why. Needless to repeat no foreign workers in the Gulf area can form or be part of a labour union.

Especially tragic was the tale of two workers from that very camp. They starved themselves in order to send home as much money as they could. Finally, unable to take the salary delays and the horrid conditions any longer, they purchased some life insurance and committed suicide. In their final notes, they requested that the insurance agent hand over the proceeds of the insurance claims directly to their families in India.

This is not uncommon. During the last three years alone, 541 low-paid Indian workers have killed themselves in the UAE, and in the same period, at least 337 Indians have died through suspected suicide in Saudi Arabia. And remember, these are just the official figures. No one knows how many other deaths are related to suicide. Other Gulf countries have also seen their annual suicide rates double in recent years as oil prices have collapsed, putting tremendous pressure on these oil-exporting economies. As government contracts are cancelled in the wake of these pressures, the private sector reels and foreign workers' salaries are the first things to be sacrificed to the bottom line.

As of this writing in 2018, the Indian government is making desperate pleas to white-collar Indians in Kuwait, Saudi Arabia, and other Gulf nations to help their less-fortunate fellow countrymen. Tens of thousands of construction workers have lost their jobs in these nations and have not received their salaries for many months. Some are homeless and starving in the sweltering desert heat. In the summer of 2016, Indian expats in Dubai made desperate attempts to provide these men with food and organize their exit visas. However, in countries like Qatar and Saudi Arabia, foreign workers are not allowed to leave the country unless their sponsor signs the necessary paperwork, which can be very difficult when the sponsoring company has folded or pulled out of the country all together. While this is not the case in Dubai, where an exit visa is not required, workers' passports are held by their employers.[20]

With all of this information, Ram was now fully armed and equipped to make his dream come true in Dubai. This is the reality he was facing in the world of petrodollars and *kafala*, the modern-day slavery system.

To my knowledge, Ram is still labouring away in the Dubai desert, hoping and praying that his sacrifice will be worth it and that he can actually make enough money for his family to get their possessions back from the moneylenders and escape the vicious cycle of poverty that has haunted them for many generations.

Too many men like Ram have come to Dubai seeking their fortune and ended up penniless, hungry, desperate, and even dead. Sheikh Mohamed and his fellow leadership team need to wake up and realize that even one death to build their glitzy skyscrapers is one too many.

---

20. You can read more about this here: https://uk.news.yahoo.com/india-says-bring-back-workers-083043422.html. Other countries like the Philipines are also working to help bring their stranded workers home: https://uk.news.yahoo.com/philippines-saudis-negotiate-over-stranded-workers-053206444.html.

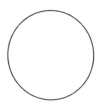

RULE OF LAW, DUBAI STYLE

It is very true that Dubai is one of the safest places in the world. Anyone can comfortably walk around wearing a 22-karat gold Rolex President bracelet at one in the morning without the slightest risk of being mugged. Dubai residents regularly go away on holiday and have no qualms about leaving their expensive cars in their parking spots on the street; no one ever touches them.

This is not only true of Dubai, but also of the entire UAE and, in fact, the entire Gulf region. In Saudi Arabia, there is a saying among the expat community: there is no need to lock up your house when going away for a holiday. No one would even dream of entering an empty house, let alone removing personal property.

In fact, Saudi Arabia is so strict about preventing and punishing theft that jokes about it have sprung up within the expat community there. One such joke is about a migrant from a poor south Asian country who was walking along the road in Riyadh, the Saudi capital. The joke goes that the laborer saw a bag, which appeared to be full of rice. As a conscientious, law-abiding individual, he took the bag to the nearest police station so that it could be returned to its lawful owners. Back in his own country, this could potentially lead to a reward from the rightful owners.

When the labourer brought the bag of rice to the Saudi police, they asked him, "Where did you find this bag?"

"On the roadside," said the man.

The Saudi policeman then reconfirmed, "And this is not your bag?"

"No sir, this bag of rice is not mine," the labourer said proudly, reaffirming his honesty.

"Then how do you know it contains rice?" asked the officer.

"Well, I poked the sack, and it felt like it had rice in it," said the Asian laborer.

"Which hand did you use to poke the bag?" asked the policeman.

"This hand, sir," confirmed the foreigner, confidently raising his right arm.

An hour later, he walked away from the police station, minus that arm. The moral of the joke is, in Saudi Arabia, do not touch something that does not belong to you.

This might just be an expat-community joke, but there are plenty of horrific, real-life stories that reflect this attitude. For example, I heard about a British couple in Saudi Arabia that reported their young Bangladeshi help to the police for some petty theft. A few days later, they were horrified to see the young man return with a bandaged stump, rather than his hand. The Saudi authorities had amputated one of his hands after he confessed to the theft. The young man had thought he would get a light reprimand if he admitted his crime and did not waste the court's time.

Saudi Arabia is universally recognized as a very strict society. Saudis make it extremely clear what will and will not be tolerated. If you are caught drinking or even transporting alcohol, you will be thrown in jail and lashed with hard cane. If you are caught fornicating outside of marriage—especially if you are a married woman—you will be stoned to death. If you are a man and you are driving a car, a woman can only sit next to you if she is your wife. If the *muttawa*, or religious police, stop you, you need to have a marriage certificate, with a legal translation into Arabic and authenticated by your embassy, on-hand in your car. It doesn't matter if the woman sitting next to you is your mother or sister—if she is not your legally married wife, you will be punished. There is no grey area in Saudi law and no question about the impact of non-compliance.

Consuming alcohol is strictly prohibited in Saudi Arabia, and many expats go over to Bahrain, where alcohol is freely available, to imbibe. On most Thursday nights, the start of the Gulf weekend, there are long queues and traffic snarls in the causeway connecting Saudi Arabia to Bahrain, caused by thirsty expats heading to the watering holes in Bahrain. Wealthy Saudis occasionally fly over to Dubai to indulge as well. As long as they do not do such things in Saudi Arabia, it's fine.

Of course, expats and Saudi locals alike take chances with the Saudi law; after all, they are only human, but they do so at their own peril. I have interviewed a number of expats there, and many of them know someone in the expat community who brews their own liquor or runs an X-rated video distribution business. They do so knowing exactly what will happen to them if any of their friends or customers ever snitches on them.

However, there are a few exclusive expat residential areas in Saudi Arabia where the posh foreigners are left to their own devices. Inside these compounds surrounded by high walls and with gated entrances—which are often owned by multinational oil firms—anything and everything is available, and parties are not for the weak-hearted. These compounds are like diplomatic enclaves in a way, and the Saudi police do not enter them unless there is a something truly serious, like a murder or terrorist attack.

Of course, Saudi locals know just how far they can push their luck. Al Jabbar, an elderly senior government official and a good acquaintance of mine in Saudi Arabia who loves his Johnny Walker Blue-Label Scotch, once boasted that his farm (they call their second homes in the desert their "farmhouses," which come fully stocked with the finest camels and date trees) in the Saudi desert has a better Scotch collection than can be found among the Scottish landed gentry in the Highlands. When in Dubai, he has at least four large pegs of whiskey every evening, and he lodges his young South Korean girlfriend in a villa in

Jumeirah, Dubai, while his wife of forty years lives in Riyadh.[21]

So yes, people do indeed take risks with Saudi law. Some do it for the adrenalin rush, some for the *fulus* (money), and some simply because it is the proverbial forbidden apple. Yet everyone who does so is fully aware of the consequences for even the slightest sign of non-compliance.

Fortunately, Dubai law is not nearly as harsh as its Saudi counterpart—at least, not on the surface. Dubai's laws are infinitely more complicated though, and if someone is down on his or her luck, dealing with the Dubai legal system can be pretty obnoxious. On the surface, Dubai is a modern, commercial, multicultural melting pot, but beneath its shiny veneer of modernity lies a completely different, complex, prehistoric monster. Behind the relative safety and security that Dubai provides is a gigantic police-state machinery run by locals at the top and by Arabic-speaking expats—mainly from Yemen and Sudan—at the bottom.

Dubai is an authoritarian police state, and its laws are very clearly designed to keep its large expatriate population on its toes. In the rest of the world, the common assumption is that laws are directed at and should be followed by everyone. In Dubai though, there seems to be two separate legal systems: one for locals and one for foreigners. Even though the local population officially falls under the same legal jurisdiction, very few, if any, get dragged into its net, and then only in cases of

---

21. This information is based on personal interviews. Names have been changed to protect the individuals' identities.

extreme behaviour, such as murder, rape, or political agitation.

It is a system in which an individual is assumed guilty until proven innocent and in which people can make malicious false complaints against their neighbours, employers, and employees as a way to punish or hurt them financially and socially for perceived wrongs. Furthermore, defendants are not guaranteed proper legal representation and the right to defend themselves.

Dubai's extensive police state infrastructure is run and supported by the *khabri* network, or the CID (Criminal Investigation Department). *Khabar* is Arabic for "news," and the *khabri* are the people who provide the news. This is an extensive population of full-time plainclothes police officers who patrol the streets in unmarked police cars, day and night.

In addition, there are voluntary CIDs that provide invaluable support to the formal, regular police force. The volunteer CIDs are drawn from a number of local populations, including:

1. Local youths from respectable families. These young men are actually given CID training and police identification badges to facilitate their stops and searches of expatriates. These part-time CIDs are not supposed to stop and search locals. They generally go around in pairs in unmarked police cars.

    Recruiting plainclothes CID volunteers from the local community has political implications as well. It is a way for Dubai's government to demonstrate its power-sharing arrangements with its citizens. It gives locals a feeling of power, as even the average young local man realizes that he has the power and the legal right to search and harass expats whenever he wishes, thus reinforcing the belief that he is superior to the expats around him, a belief which has been ingrained in him since birth. In addition, serving as voluntary CIDs keeps the younger generation gainfully occupied so that they aren't thinking about things like human rights, revolution, and uprisings, as we saw in other countries during the Arab Spring.

2. The next group of informal, but very effective, CIDs comes from within the foreign expat community itself. Every single residential apartment building across the UAE has a caretaker, known as a *nathur*. A *nathur* is a resident caretaker, guard, and cleaner all rolled into one, and he is there twenty-four hours a day. His primary function is to show empty apartments to prospective tenants and provide existing tenants with the owner's contact information when needed for things like rent contracts.

*Nathur*s are very effective at providing information to the police, due to the nature of their work. They know things like who is coming and going from their building, whether a single man is bringing in women, whether a tenant is behaving suspiciously, and even whether a couple is fighting. All of this information is passed on to the local youths entrusted with CID work. It keeps the Dubai police informed about the activities and movements of every single foreigner in the city.

As a result, the Dubai police know everything about

the city's foreign residents: who goes to the weekly fish markets, who goes to pray and where and when, who brings alcohol back to their residence, or any other vital information that may be relevant for a criminal investigation, such as an accusation of flipping someone off or having sex outside of marriage.

3. The next group of informants are Dubai taxi drivers, foreigners once again. Whereas *nathur*s provide a static set of data about the residents of a building, taxi drivers provide mobile information about Dubai's foreign residents. Taxi drivers are in a position to tell the police who is going where and when, whether a couple was trying to touch each other in the back of the cab, whether a couple was discussing something in hushed tones—which may pertain to drugs or alcohol—who was drunk, and other such vital intelligence.

   At times, they may pick up slightly tipsy expat men and, much more rarely, women and simply drive them straight to the police station. Sometimes, they will engage in a fare dispute and bring them to a police station to "resolve the dispute," where the ever-grateful policemen, waiting for "business," charge the passenger with disturbing public order and instantly lock them up. After all, every police station has a target quota to meet. It is best for foreign Dubai residents to avoid any form of verbal dispute with a Dubai taxi driver.

4. The final group of unofficial Dubai *khabri*s are the city's municipal workers who are mostly foreigners

themselves. In addition to collecting rubbish or cleaning the roads, these workers keep a sharp lookout for the slightest disturbance being caused by expats. They have been known to stand as independent witnesses in many frivolous cases against other expats.

All four types of unofficial intelligence providers are strictly advised not to interfere with local men or women. Foreigners, however, are fair game and their only target.

In a personal interview, Sachin Singh of New Delhi, India, told me what happened to him when he came to Dubai to work for Emirates NBD Banking Group. Like many expats, Singh had left a highflying corporate career in his home country to come to Dubai. Headhunted by the Emirates NBD Group, he was attracted to Dubai by to its tax-free, hard-currency, US-dollar linked salary and the belief that he was getting an exciting international career break. Used to highflying corporate parties and events in India's super-deluxe hotels, a privilege of the very few in that country, Singh believed he could continue his glamourous lifestyle in Dubai with even greater ease. After all, he now had more disposable income, due to the lack of personal taxes.

One night, Singh went out with a few other Indian bachelor friends. Like him, they were all professionals working in management positions in respectable businesses. There are no restrictions for non-Muslims on drinking alcohol in Dubai restaurants, and one weekend, they headed to Pur Dubai, the old part of the town, for a few drinks and a meal. Afterwards, they left the restaurant and started strolling along and chatting among themselves amiably. It was around ten pm on a Thursday night—the start of the Gulf weekend—so it was certainly not considered late yet.

Suddenly, a white Toyota Corolla pulled up in front of this group, and two young locals got out. They rudely asked the group for their IDs. Once their IDs were verified, the two men started interrogating the group, asking where they were going and what they were doing. After further thorough scrutiny of their papers and more very intrusive and insulting interrogation, these men started screaming at the group that they had to go back home immediately, as though they were a serious risk to peace and public order. Once the young men left, the group quickly hailed a taxi and went home, quite shaken and humiliated. They felt that they had been treated like some uncouth hooligans and criminals.

The next day at work, Singh described his ordeal to a very good friend and colleague, Jafar al Bannai, who was a UK-educated local. Modern, enlightened al Bannai's immediate response to that bizarre event was, "Were you guys drunk?" Singh assured him that they were not, and al Bannai told his friend that he was very lucky, because under such situations, CID agents have the power to arrest them and take them to a police station for overnight detention. They even have the power to detain anyone they wish for a couple of days; when released from custody, the employer or the sponsor could very well deport the individual for drunken behavior without any further ado.

Al Bannai then elaborated on the backgrounds of these young men, who were generally the teenage children of influential locals. They are provided with police ID and the authority to stop, search, and arrest foreigners. He also reminded his friend that the Dubai government targets foreign single males—particularly if they are in a large group—more proactively than foreign families. The government believes that families pose a far lower security risk than single men. Hearing all this, Singh vowed to never go out with his bachelor friends in Dubai again.

This was not an isolated incident for him, though. One evening, Singh was walking from his apartment to a friend's car. They were planning to drive over to another friend's house to have dinner together. Suddenly, two white Toyota Corollas pulled up and blocked their car's passage, and four young local men rushed out of the cars, screaming as if they were trying to stop a bank-robbery getaway vehicle. Both Singh and his friend were hauled out of the car, and the CIDs thoroughly searched it, especially the glove compartment. They appeared to be searching for something specific and were truly disappointed not to have found it.

Singh and his friend did have some Bollywood movie DVDs with them that they were planning to watch later that evening. Having failed to find what they hoped to, the CIDs showed special interest in the discs, hoping that they had caught two Asian men with pornographic material. What they were really looking for was a drug bust. If they had found drugs, they would have hit the jackpot in terms of their policing efforts. Failing that, these young CIDs were hoping for the consolation prize of catching two immigrants with X-rated videos in their possession. When they realized that the DVDs were innocent Bollywood movies, the CID grudgingly let Singh and his friend go.

When he related this incident to his local friend in the office the next day, al Bannai told him that this was a very normal "stop and search" practice. The CID, it seems, must have been keeping a watch on some apartments in that area, looking for suspected drug trafficking or prostitution. It seems that this "stop and search" of any foreigner was the best way to track down the culprits.

A few years later, when Singh was engaged, he took his fiancée out for a meal at the Hyatt Dubai and was confronted in the hotel parking lot by two young local males. The two locals asked for their ID papers, but by now, Singh had been in Dubai for several years and was far wiser regarding how the local law enforcement worked. He plucked up sufficient courage to ask these two young men for their police ID instead and then questioned why were they following and harassing him.

The young men responded, "You are out with a lady, and we do not believe she is your wife." Then they demanded that both Singh and his fiancée come with them to the Bur Dubai police station. Singh readily agreed, which seemed to fluster the young men. They began talking to each other in Arabic, then returned the couple's IDs and sped off in their unmarked Toyota Corolla.

It should be mentioned that the head of a police station is called the *Mudir Al Alam*, Arabic for "General Manager," and the next-most-senior policeman is known as the *Mudir*, or "Manager." A police station's organizational structure is similar to that of a profit-driven private enterprise. According to a number of my business associates who work closely with the Dubai police, the Key Performance Indicator (KPI) for employees (the policemen) is how many foreigners they can lock up and charge with crimes. The stations are understood to have targets or quotas of how many individuals—specifically, foreigners—they can lock up.

These same sources also say that police officers' bonuses are directly tied to the number and types of crimes they are able to book and the level of convictions they are able to secure. A drug haul or a drug-use conviction are the highest in the pecking order, and any Dubai police officer or police station would give an arm and a leg to get such a crime on their books. Thus, police officers are highly incentivized to make any kind of drug bust they can, whether it be few grams of marijuana or a large container of cocaine. If a person is caught with more than a few grams of marijuana (the exact measurement allowed is difficult to determine, and accurate information is not available to the public), the consequences are crystal clear: the choice of execution by either firing squad or hanging.

Failing that, catching a rapist or a sexual offender can also be highly lucrative for the police. The term "sexual offender" has a very different meaning in the UAE than in many other countries, especially those in the West. In the UAE, if a woman reports that she has been raped, she can immediately be taken into custody and counter-charged with "sexual activity outside of matrimony," a jailable offense in Dubai. According to the Emirates Centre for Human Rights, UAE law states that a rape conviction can only be secured after a confession or as the result of testimony from four adult male witnesses to the crime, making such a conviction almost impossible. As a result, women must be very wary about making any such criminal complaints in the UAE.[22]

In general, these "sex criminals" are almost always foreigners. There are plenty of cases of testosterone-driven local teenagers raping their family's Filipina or sub-Saharan maid; however, the local family generally uses its *wasta* (influence and connections) to free the criminal long before the case ever reaches court. In addition, expats and foreigners rarely dare complain about criminal wrongdoing by locals; they are too scared of the

---

22. In November 2016, a British woman complained to the Dubai Police that she was gang-raped, and she was immediately arrested on charges of sex outside marriage. See: www.independent.co.uk/news/uk/home-news/british-woman-tourist-arrested-charged-jail-dubai-gang-rape-extra-marital-sex-hotel-uae-police-a7420616.html. Similarly, in July 2013, the BBC reported that Norwegian citizen Marta Dalelv, an interior designer, was on a business trip in Dubai when she reported to the police that she had been raped. She was immediately arrested on grounds of sex outside of marriage, drinking alcohol, and perjury. She was sentenced to sixteen months in prison for these charges: www.bbc.co.uk/news/world-middle-east-23381448.This sort of thing happens not only in Dubai, but all across the Gulf countries. In Qatar, a Norwegian woman reported being raped and was immediately arrested under suspicion of adultery: https://uk.news.yahoo.com/dutch-woman-held-qatar-over-rape-complaint-123508727.html.

potential consequences.

In general, the police and court systems are designed to control the behaviour of foreigners, and the police only receive financial bonuses when they catch and are able to convict a foreigner of a crime. As a result, every year, hundreds—possibly even thousands—of foreigners are subjected to a terrible and harsh process of complete vilification by a system that is renowned for its gross human rights violations. Most people who are forced to deal with the Dubai justice system do so based on truly frivolous and laughable charges that would be considered ridiculous and total waste of police times in most other countries in this world.

For example, in November 2017, British expat Asa Hutchinson was arrested and charged with "witnessing a fight." Several of her friends were visiting her in Dubai when they got in to an altercation with another man. That man reported the incident to the police, but since her friends had already left Dubai, the police charged her because she had witnessed the fight. This story also reveals another interesting facet of the criminal justice system in the Gulf: the police generally believe whoever complains first.[23]

Another "serious crime" in Dubai is having a returned check, and check defaulters are brought to court in tight metal cages fitted to the backs of small vans, much like how police

---

23. You can read Hutchinson's full story here: www.msn.com/en-gb/news/world/british-woman-21-arrested-in-dubai-for-witnessing-fight-in-hotel-lobby/ar-BBFUk7V?li=BBoPRmx&ocid=UP97DHP.

dogs are brought to a crime scene. In fact, far more people are imprisoned for writing checks that bounce than for all other criminal offenses—such as rape, robbery, or murder—put together. However, these days, only expats can be considered check defaulters, as, in 2015, the law was changed to preclude locals from being charged with a crime if they happen to write a check that bounces.

To really see that compliance with the law is only required of expats and foreigners, one simply has to make a short visit to Dubai's most dreaded and infamous institution: the Dubai Prosecutor's Office. It occupies a substantial part of the main Dubai Court Building. What stands out the most about this institution is the fact that practically everyone that attends that court are expats. Every day, hundreds of foreigners trudge to this court simply because someone has complained to the police about them. They can be summoned to court for the pettiest of complaints or on the flimsiest of grounds. Charges can include things like, "He said bad words to me," "He was shouting at the taxi driver in public," or the very serious crime of showing someone the middle finger.

In most other countries in the world, the defendant is assumed innocent until proven guilty. In the UAE, however, the defendant is assumed guilty until proven innocent. In addition, there is very little difference between the civil law and criminal law.

Prosecutors are generally the crème-de-la-crème of UAE society, and they are nearly always well-connected locals. They are given the power to punish a defendant before they even appear in the main court and are proven guilty. Therefore, the prosecutor's office is very aptly dubbed "the Court of First Instance," because the prosecutors use their power to immediately punish anybody who appears before them. In the initial stages of any case, however frivolous, the prosecutors are the judge, jury, and jailor all rolled into one.

While prosecutors are almost always locals, the judges are sometimes Arabic-speaking foreigners, such as Palestinian or Egyptian nationals. Local prosecutors do not want to take any chances with these judges, as they aren't sure whether they will free the defendant, who is generally a foreigner, due to their "liberal" views and interpretations of the law. Thus, this is further motivation for them to punish defendants before producing them in court.

This kind of punishment usually entails holding the defendant in judicial custody for many months before producing them in court—even for the pettiest of 'crimes' and on the mere suspicions or allegations. During some periods of the year, like at Ramadan, Independence Day, and various national holidays, judicial incarceration can last even longer, because the court systems are backed up due to shorter working hours.

This is the fate that Sanjay Gambhir, who ran a very successful commercial brokerage firm in Dubai, narrowly escaped. During an interview, he explained to me that he had had serious marital problems, and his wife eventually left him, taking all their household goods with her, and moved in with another man in Dubai. She then began a vile campaign of terror against him, calling his business associates and spreading vicious rumors about him. Everyone understood that she was trying to maximize her divorce settlement, but eventually Gambhir decided that enough was enough. He hired a lawyer to talk to his ex-wife, but the harassment only grew worse. When he asked his lawyer for advice, he suggested that Gambhir make a token complaint to the local police station to rein her in. Unfortunately, this set off a chain reaction that soon turned into Gambhir's worst nightmare.

In order to deflect attention from her own "serious crime"—the fact that she was now living in an adulterous relationship with her new boyfriend, a very serious crime in Dubai that could even lead to the death penalty—his wife claimed that she was not actually his wife. The Dubai police charged both Gambhir and his wife with illegal cohabitation outside marriage, made them sign various documents in Arabic, and handed the matter over to the Dubai Court of First Instance.

Gambhir reported to the prosecutor's office as ordered and sat down in the reception area with his lawyer. He had never faced a situation like this before; in fact, he had never even been near a police station before. Now he suddenly found himself charged with a fairly serious crime by local standards, all because he had sought support from local law enforcement because his personal life and his business were being seriously disturbed. He had been warned that making any kind of complaint to the police could easily lead to a visit to the prosecutor's office as a defendant himself, but Gambhir, a highly educated, successful businessman, had a hard time believing that a person could truly be detained for merely asking the police for protection.

Until now.

The prosecutor's office waiting area was swarming with police officers. In fact, the entire area was very secure, fortified by iron gates and guarded by numerous policemen. When the defendant's name was called, they went into the courtroom through those iron gates and did not return.

It was a very hot day in May, and the heat, the stress of the situation, and the atmosphere of fear that permeated the building made Gambhir feel sick. Though he believed in God, he was not normally a religious man, but at that moment, he started chanting sacred words. He was not alone in this. All around him, foreigners from different religious backgrounds were sweating and praying. Some fingered religious beads, while others prayed silently and cursed themselves for the greed that had brought them to Dubai in the first place.

Soon, a policeman bellowed Gambhir's name, and he sprang to attention. He and his lawyer, who was charging him an exorbitant fee, strode into the prosecutor's office. As he crossed the iron gates, he noticed one of the policemen guarding them eye his gold Rolex watch. Unbidden, the thought arose, *If money can prevent prison rape in a foreign jail by asking for police protection, then so be it.*

As Gambhir and his lawyer went further down the corridor, he saw countless empty cells—judicial lock-ups—and wondered which one would be his residence that night.

Another policeman ushered them into a chamber. Sitting at the end of the room in a central position were two local men, one of whom Gambhir rightly guessed was the prosecutor.

The prosecutor did not look at him; by law, the judge and the prosecutor—who is also the judge in the Court of First Instance—is not allowed to make eye contact with any of the parties present: defendant, plaintiff, or witnesses from either side to ensure UAE-style fair play.

The other man was the translator, and the prosecutor addressed all questions to him, who in turn relayed them to Gambhir in Hindi/Urdu. To his surprise, his lawyer just sat there quietly the whole time. The prosecutor did not address any questions to the lawyer, nor did the lawyer volunteer anything, ask any questions himself, or deflect any line of questioning from the prosecutor. He seemed to be nothing more than a silent observer.

The prosecutor's questions were extremely personal and intrusive: Do you have a marriage certificate? What is your religion? What religious ceremony did you follow when you got married? Do you have a photograph of your marriage ceremony? Where did you get married? Do you have any children out of the wedlock? And the main question: did you have sex with your wife? For more than an hour, he was grilled about every aspect of his marriage and sex life.

Finally, the prosecutor addressed his lawyer in Arabic. From his limited grasp of the language, Gambhir understood that the prosecutor was asking for a copy of his marriage certificate authenticated by the Indian Embassy in Dubai.

After that, the prosecutor asked him why his wife had left him and what the reason was for their initial dispute. Through all this, he hardly touched on the nature of Gambhir's original complaint: that his wife was disturbing his life and business, despite having walked away with all of his possessions and a significant amount of cash from their home.

Finally, the prosecutor told his lawyer something in Arabic, and his lawyer told Gambhir, "Let's go." They left the prosecutor's area, and Gambhir, the plaintiff, could not believe his good fortune: he was walking away from the Dubai prosecutor's office as a free man! Never before had anything like this ever happened to a foreigner in Dubai.

As they walked back through the corridors, Gambhir saw that the empty cells were quickly filling up with people he recognized from the reception area earlier. He did not tarry to look back at them, but rather scampered out of the building.

Nearly everyone who goes to the prosecutor's office does not return home that night, and when they do return, it is with a criminal record. So how was it that Gambhir was set free? His innocence certainly had nothing to do with it, since he was a foreigner. Was it the obscene amount of money he had paid his lawyer? Was it his gold Rolex watch, since in Dubai, people who are perceived to be rich are also perceived to be above the law? Did his local sponsor use his *wasta*, fearing that if Gambhir was jailed or detained, his monthly cash flow would crumble? Or was it that the policemen had watered down the original police report because he had helped them in the past? Ultimately, Gambhir did not know, and he did not care. All that mattered to him was that he was a free man.

Even when foreigners are able to avoid being detained, it can take months or even years to be fully free of the court system.

During that time, the foreigner's passport can and will legally be held by the police.

In a personal interview, Perry Dubey told me what happened when some disgruntled employees who were trying to extort money from him accused him of cursing. The accusation was made at the end of the month of Ramadan and the beginning of Eid, a period of prolonged national holidays when the court system moves particularly slowly. This was done on purpose, since it meant that the police would have no other option but to hold him in custody for at least ten days before producing him at the prosecutor's office. Dubey's accusers thought that this would leave him demoralized, scared, and perfectly happy to give in to their illicit monetary demands—which would be extortion in any normal society. This kind of extortion is not uncommon in Dubai, where the unscrupulous use the state apparatus to ruin people's lives, reputations, and livelihoods in order to make money, is quite common.

Fortunately, Dubey as a businessman , had his passport on-hand, as well as that of another employee of his, and given the silly nature of the accusations and his own *wasta*, the police let him go home that very night, so long as he surrendered his passport and that of his employee. He was out of the police station within an hour, and his accusers were greatly dismayed. One even called his residence anonymously from a local phone booth the next morning to find out whether he was languishing in the Murragabat police lock-up. Instead, on learning that he had been sleeping comfortably in his king-sized bed in his large apartment with central air conditioning, the caller was extremely outraged.

A few weeks later, certain of his innocence and swift vindication, Dubey reported to the Dubai Courts as ordered. There, the judge demanded again and again, "Did you do this? Did you use bad words?" despite Dubey's consistent denial of the charges. Eventually, tired of the defendant's denials, the judge ordered him into a large cage on the courtroom's right-hand side. Dubey knew then that he had been convicted of cursing. Why else would the judge send him into the cage where all the "convicted" were waiting?

Once inside the cage, he turned around and saw the people who had come with him to court as moral support—his brother and his office assistant—look completely crestfallen. They quietly left the courtroom, also convinced that he had been convicted and that there was nothing they could do to save him. For his part, Dubey resigned himself to spending at least a couple weeks in jail.

As soon as the court sessions were over for the day, all of the prisoners were herded downstairs to a very secure area with steel doors. Quite a few men, most of them check defaulters, were desperately trying to call their friends, relatives, or lawyers in sheer panic while they still had their mobile phones.

Dubey still could not believe what was happening. It was only when the men were ushered into an even-more-secure area did the enormity of the situation finally dawn on him: for the first time in his life, he was in jail. He would now have a criminal record, and to make matters worse, it was all based on some trumped-up charges from people who were trying to extort money from him.

The wait in that secure holding area was excruciating. More and more "convicted criminals" were being brought in from other parts of the court. Many men were huddled together, muttering things like, "There are no human rights here," "The UAE is the worst place in the world," "Never confess to what they allege," "Be very careful what you say here, because there are *khabris*/CIDs everywhere."

Dubey realized just how serious the situation was when a few of the men started winking at him. He began to mutter prayers and steeled himself to resist any form of prison assault that he might be subjected to.

He was expecting his name to be called at any minute and then be taken away to a proper jail cell, so he was quite surprised when a policeman came in with a white sheet of paper, called out, "Dubey Perry ? Dubey Perry ? Come here. Come on out," and opened the locked iron gates for him.

As he exited the enclosure, he saw his brother and office assistant standing nearby wearing huge smiles. "You're innocent! You're innocent!" they shouted.

The policeman did not like the well-wishers' jubilant spirits; he informed Dubey that he was free to go and had him sign a document, which was, of course, in Arabic. Dubey gleefully signed it, just thrilled to be released.

He and his entourage then hurried past several groups of police officers without even a parting glance for Dubey's fellow accused. It may have been selfish, but the quicker the getaway from that hell hole, the better. It was only when he reached his car that Dubey realized that the wait inside the secured area was a part of Dubai's legal process. The paperwork proclaiming his innocence was being processed while he was left to socialize with potential convicted rapists.

Dubey now thought that he was home free and cleared of all charges. However, his ordeal was far from over.

A few weeks later, Dubey received a letter from the Dubai court system, ordering him to attend Dubai's Supreme Court in one month on the same charges of cursing. Apparently, the prosecutor had appealed the lower court's innocent verdict, so now there would be a second hearing.

In the month that followed, Dubey's business prospects grew considerably worse due to his pending charges. His small firm's business had come to a stand-still, and everything was in state of uncertainty. He could not travel for business, no one wanted to finalize business transactions with him, there was no possibility of hiring another much-needed employee, and there was absolutely no chance of being able to borrow funds to temporarily improve the firm's liquidity to get them through this crisis. At the same time, all overhead costs still had to be covered: salaries and rent had to be paid, or else additional criminal charges would be laid against him.

His previous lawyer now requested truly extortionate fees, so Dubey looked for another one, only to be met with equally outrageous fees wherever he called. One lawyer said outright that he would not take the case, "Because the prosecution apparently was losing this case." This was a truly exceptional thing, as the Dubai prosecution almost never lost. If the Supreme Court also sided with Dubey and set him free, the Dubai prosecutor would remember the lawyer who helped him and consequently punish all his future clients by putting them in jail.

His many business associates and contacts in Dubai assured him that this was a very normal practice here. One urged him not to worry, because even if he was convicted, all the court would do was either give him a paltry fine or incarcerate him for seven days. Still, Dubey was shocked. *Seven days in jail for a false and malicious complaint about cursing intended to extort money from me?* he thought.

All of this, coupled with the extreme mental distress and shame, left him seriously mulling suicide. On his assigned court date, Dubey returned to the same courtroom and once again faced the same scenario. Once again, the judge demanded, "Is this true? Have you said bad words?"

This time though, Dubey decided to take matters into his own hands. Instead of answering the question through an interpreter, he turned directly to the judge and, being an educated man, addressed him in English. "Your honour, sir," he began, and then started to give his side of the story and explain the situation.

On being addressed in English, the judge looked up from the mound of papers in front of him in surprise, but then immediately looked away again. Ruffled, the judge asked the translator to again ask Dubey whether he had done what he was being accused of and to answer only "Yes" or "No." Exasperated, Dubey said "No" as emphatically, clearly, and loudly as he could in a courtroom without sounding rude.

The judge then began writing something, possibly the judgment, when a hawkish-looking local sitting to the right of the judge, presumably a prosecutor, stood up and started shouting in Arabic. A brief exchange ensued between the two men in Arabic, after which the judge stopped writing and spoke to the translator. The embarrassed-looking translator, a policeman in uniform, told Dubey that he needed to come back to this same courtroom at the same time the following week.

When he exited the courtroom, one of his well-wishers who understood Arabic informed Dubey that the judge had been about to release him fully, but the local prosecutor had started insisting that Dubey was a "bad man" and that he was going to present additional evidence of this. The judge had no other option but to listen to the local prosecutor and reschedule Dubey for another court date.

Having finished this latest instalment of his ordeal, Dubey headed straight to his local bar to quench his thirst on this hot desert afternoon and drown his frustrations and worries about his future. The one bright light in all this darkness was that his business had sufficient liquidity for the moment and that he had no outstanding checks in the marketplace that could potentially bounce and make him an actual, and even bigger, criminal in the eyes of the Dubai judicial system.

A week later, Dubey again returned to court. By now, he recognized a few of the faces around him. The same routine ensued, with the judge asking questions in Arabic and the translator, who was a uniformed policeman, translating them into the defendant's language. This whole time, the judge never once made eye contact with the various defendants. After an hour, during which Dubey was never called, the judge read out two lists in Arabic, then stood up and regally strode out of the courtroom. The translator clicked his heels in respect, stood at military attention, and saluted the judge as he swept out of the court room, as though he were a president or prime minister.

Dubey did not know what was going on, and he was naturally very tense and nervous. Suddenly, the policeman standing near the cage shouted his name and pointed toward the cage. Dubey assumed he had been convicted, and his stomach fell. He walked to the cage, hoping against hope that, like the last time, he would just be waiting for his "innocence papers" to be processed.

After about fifteen minutes, the policeman opened the door of the cage and read out a list of approximately a dozen names, one of which was Dubey's. Many of the men in this group were clearly locals. Knowing that, in Dubai, locals were almost never actually convicted of a crime, Dubey's mind was immediately put at ease. He was among men who were surely declared innocent. This group was shepherded out of the cage and across the courtroom in a single-file line. With a police escort, they set off for another secure building behind the main court building. As they marched along, the local men were all smiles; they knew exactly what was happening.

Their destination was the administrative wing of the criminal court system, which was managed by young local men who were extremely rude. As Dubey waited for his release papers, one such clerk asked him if he knew how lucky he was to escape being locked up.

After a few hours of anxious waiting, Dubey received his release papers, which were, of course, in Arabic, and was told to get lost. The clerk was clearly angry that an Indian man was going free without a criminal conviction on his records.

Dubey did not have to be told twice. He grabbed his release papers, jumped into a cab, and headed straight to the Marriot Hotel for a celebratory drink. He was a bit worried that the case might have turned him into an alcoholic, based on the quantity of alcohol he had consumed during its course, but at the moment, he didn't really care.

The next day, he went to the Murragabat police station in Deira with his "innocence papers" to retrieve his passport. Unfortunately, the police said that this was just a court verdict, and now he had to wait for a special letter from the prosecutor's office to get his passport back, which was expected to take another few weeks. The policeman who had started the so-called investigation told him in broken English that, if he wanted to, Dubey could start a case against his ex-employees who had lodged the initial complaint, against him in retaliation.

Considering the option, Dubey wondered how many more years of his life he would spend embroiled in court cases if should he do so. He ultimately decided against it and to just focus his efforts on getting his passport back. He enquired how he could fast-track his passport release, and a foreigner in the police department told him that, in all likelihood, it could take months for the prosecution to release his passport; they were likely to be upset at their inability to punish him with even a token fine, so they would drag their feet on this in retaliation. It would be up to his drive, initiative, contacts, and *wasta* to get his passport back. That is exactly what he did, and Dubey got his passport back in a record seven days.

If it takes nearly four months to get through a false complaint from fellow foreigners in the courts, imagine what it takes to get through a returned check case or a complaint lodged by a local sponsor about a business dispute. The Dubai courts can suck away months and even years from the accused.

While foreigners can be held for an extended period of time for truly minor things, locals are only subjected to the full legal process for the most heinous of crimes. For example, a local can and will be prosecuted if they murder another local. In the late 1990s, there was only one slot machine in the UAE (in an Ajman pub that I frequented when I went to the beach there), because gambling is strictly banned. One night, two locals came to blows during an argument about their winnings. The argument led to murder, and the murderer was prosecuted. After this, the room housing the slot machine was locked up. When I asked what had caused this, the owner told me the whole story.

There is also a traditional custom that has been enshrined in the law that allows a local to literally get away with murder and not face prosecution. This is the practice of offering *diya*, or blood money, to the family of the deceased. If the victim's family accepts it, the murderer can resume his normal, day-to-day life without any further consequences.

The state regularly uses torture to extract confessions of wrongdoing from foreigners. In a serious murder or drug charge, suspects are tortured until the so-called criminals confess to their crimes. If the suspect is indeed innocent and the real criminal is caught, the original suspect is simply released and told to go home, as if nothing had happened. The suspect's physical and mental trauma is simply considered a part of the normal legal and living process in Dubai. There is no apology and no concern for human rights.[24]

This is what happened to Javed Khan, the branch manager of the Gulf East Bank[25] at the Fish Roundabout in Deira, Dubai. During an interview, he told me how, one afternoon, after the bank had closed for the day, which occurs at two pm, it was discovered that there was a cash shortage in one of the branch's tills. The bank's head office immediately informed the police.

The plainclothes CID immediately came to the branch, picked up the manager, and took him to the police station's interrogation quarters. They began quizzing him, and after an hour of his repeating that he knew nothing about the missing money, they started physically abusing him. The young CID officers began to slap and hit this respectable middle-aged family man who had loyally served the bank and Dubai for more than a decade. Khan didn't know how to handle this situation.

After a few hours of this harassment, it suddenly stopped and the officers said that he could go. He returned home

---

24. You can read more about the UAE's horrific torture practices to get a better understanding of the scale of the human rights violations in the UAE on Amnesty International's website.

25. Name has been changed.

humiliated, ashamed, and literally red-faced from the strikes he had received. Shortly after he got home, he received a call from his branch deputy. Apparently, while Khan was enjoying the pleasantries of a Dubai police station, a cashier in the branch realized that he had accidentally made an excess payment to a business customer. When the cashier called the customer, the customer confirmed the excess payment and came back to the branch to return the extra cash.

There was, of course, neither an apology to Khan from the bank, nor from the police.

Another example of this is what happened to Adris Wali, a Bangladeshi who had spent many years in the Gulf and was in charge of the Northern Bank's[26] Al Deira Road branch. This branch happened to handle part of the Dubai Police Force's salary payments. As a result, it was branch practice to deliver a statement of the police force's accounts to a police messenger every day around midday. No one really checked these statements though, because they were also updated online.

Wali told me how, one afternoon, two hours after the statement was handed over, several police officers came to the bank to pick him up and take him to the station, where he was detained because there were discrepancies on the police salary account statement. The more he tried to explain that he had nothing to do with the figures on the statement, more they heckled and bullied him. They kept insisting that he had gotten into the account and pocketed a large sum of money.

---

26. Name has been changed.

Wali felt particularly betrayed because he had been dealing with these men for the past ten years. They had a cordial, even friendly, relationship. Besides, what kind of fool would fiddle with the police salary account in a vicious police state?

Just as they were preparing to lock Wali up as "a guest of the government of Dubai," they suddenly changed course and told him that he could go. Apparently, it was revealed that someone from another police station had made an accounting error.

As a middle-aged man suffering from hypertension, Wali left the police station feeling particularly unwell, and soon after, he suffered a stroke. Again, there was no apology from the police, men whom he had counted as friends and customers for many years.

The UAE, and hence Dubai as well, prides itself on being an international melting pot with citizens from all over the world calling it their temporary home. However, since the larger world is not exclusively comprised of heterosexual people, this means that members of the LGBT community have also moved to and called Dubai home at least for a time or transit through Dubai. Unfortunately, Dubai, like many Middle Eastern nations, has a very homophobic culture. In fact, in all the Gulf nations, homosexuality is a crime, which some say is punishable by death.

Lee Charlton, his husband, Jason, and their son, Kieran, were travelling on an Emirates Airlines flight to Dubai from London, where they were catching a connecting flight to South Africa. At the Dubai airport, they were detained without explanation for two hours after the woman at the check-in counter quizzically enquired if the couple were brothers. When they explained that they were a married couple, they were initially laughed at, and then escorted away. They were able to make their connecting flight, but not without considerable humiliation and stress.[27]

In a similar situation, YouTuber Gigi Gorgeous was detained at the Dubai airport for five hours for being transgender. Dubai's law explicitly forbids "the imitation of a woman by a man."[28]

Even the suspicion of homosexuality can be enough to get one in trouble. In October 2017, Jamie Harron was on a two-day stopover in Dubai on his way back home to Scotland from Afghanistan where he had been employed. He was arrested in a nightclub when it was alleged that he had touched another man's hip. Harron explained that he had just attempted to steady himself and avoid spilling his drink when he brushed past the man. Still, he was prosecuted and jailed for three months, despite the fact that the man who initially accused Harron soon withdrew his complaint. Harron lost his job and incurred thousands of pounds in legal fees. He was released only after his family in the UK raised a huge outcry via social media, which started affecting Dubai's tourism. Sheikh Mohamed himself

27. You can read the full story here: www.independent.co.uk/news/world/ middle-east/gay-couple-humiliated-after-emirates-staff-ask-if-they-are-brothers-a7083571.html.

28. You can read more about it here: https://uk.news.yahoo.com/youtuber-gigi-gorgeous-detained-dubai-154138500.html.

intervened to order Harron's release.[29]

It is important to note that part of why the sheikh intervened and had Harron released is because the man was a white UK national; it is highly unlikely that the same thing would have happened if the accused were from a developing nation or even a UK national with different skin pigment. In Dubai, where all foreigners are considered to lesser beings than the locals, there is still a pecking order for foreigners. Nationals from countries whose currencies are stronger and have a substantial white population, and from where the sheikhs buy their guns and bombs, are accorded more rights and respect. The UK and the USA are at the top of this pecking order.

Another highly sensitive issue that could mean life or death in Dubai is drugs. Drugs of any kind are illegal in Dubai, and possession of even the smallest trace amounts of narcotics can carry a heavy penalty.

In January 2018, Briton Perry Coppins spent five weeks in jail when Dubai customs officials determined that he was carrying too many prescription medications, despite the fact that such medications are completely legal in Dubai and that he was on a six-month trip and needed that extra supply of pills to treat his cancer. Not only was he thrown in jail, he was denied his medication, which triggered bouts of blindness, withdrawal symptoms, weight loss, and hallucinations. It was a near-death

---

29. You can read more about Harron's case here: www.msn.com/en-gb/news/world/no-one-should-go-through-what-ive-been-through-says-briton-jailed-for-touching-mans-hip-in-dubai/ar-AAtYg2F?li.

situation, and Coppins nearly went bankrupt from the legal fees. He was finally freed because of the attention from the international media.[30]

Similarly, in May 2017, Briton Caren Harmon was on an Emirates Airlines flight to Dubai to catch a connecting flight to Johannesburg, South Africa. When the aircraft landed in Dubai, the airline staff pointed her out to the police in black uniform, who immediately hauled her off to a detention center. Apparently, the airline staff had suspected Harmon of taking cocaine because she had a runny nose and because she kept looking into her handbag. She was only released after blood tests revealed that she was not using cocaine. Then, before her three-and-half-hour nightmare was over, she had another heart-stopping moment when the authorities informed her that the sleeping pills she had taken during the flight could land her in jail for several years if she had used them without a prescription.[31]

Given that this is what happens when you are wrongly suspected of carrying banned drugs, you can imagine what happens when an individual is actually carrying a controlled substance, even in incredibly small amounts.

---

30. You can read the details of Coppins' case here: www.theguardian.com/world/2018/jan/07/dubai-drops-charges-against-briton-detained-over-cancer-pills.

31. You can read Harmon's full story here: www.msn.com/en-gb/news/uknews/british-businesswoman-with-runny-nose-detained-at-dubai-airport-after-being-falsely-accused-of-taking-cocaine-on-Emirates.

Keith Brown, a Council Youth Officer from England, was travelling back home to the UK from Ethiopia through Dubai when customs officials stopped him in the airport. They had detected a speck of cannabis weighing .003 grams–so small that it was invisible to the naked human eye and weighing less than a grain of sugar–on the tread of one of his shoes. He likely picked it up by accident while walking around in Ethiopia. Mr. Brown was arrested and sentenced to four years in prison. As of this writing, he is still in prison, and the social media uproar has not yet succeeded in freeing him.

Robert Dalton from Gravesend, near London, was arrested upon his arrival in Dubai when 0.03 grams of cannabis was found in the bottom pocket of his old jeans. His friends said he did not use drugs, but did occasionally go clubbing. He was found guilty and sentenced to four years in jail.[32]

There are also reports of a Swiss man having been jailed when Dubai authorities found three poppy seeds in his clothing from a roll he had eaten in Heathrow before travelling to Dubai.[33]

All of these incidents are due to the fact that customs officials in Dubai use highly sensitive equipment to conduct very thorough and intrusive searches on individuals. These are then backed up by blood and urine tests to determine if there is even a trace of any banned substances within the person's system. Possession of these substances, however miniscule, garners a

---

32. You can read the full story here: http://news.bbc.co.uk/1/hi/7234786.stm.

33. You can read the full story here: http://news.bbc.co.uk/1/hi/7234786.stm.

mandatory four-year prison term.[34]

Most foreigners who live in the UAE and have had to deal with the UAE's legal system find it difficult to cope with life in the UAE afterwards. Many soon return to their home countries, utterly humiliated by their experiences and too ashamed to talk about their ordeals. This reticence does a great disservice to those who are considering moving to Dubai, as it keeps vital information from them about what life is really like there. In addition, many expats leave Dubai when they are in legal trouble, often leaving behind millions of dirhams that they have invested in their businesses in Dubai. They return to their home countries with almost nothing to show for their many years of hard work in the desert.

There are many unscrupulous locals who know this and use their positions and connections to actively try to drive away foreigners who are just asking for their legitimate dues. One example of this is Brigadier Gamma Jamman, a senior police officer in Dubai. At one point, he had been the Head of Dubai Immigration, but was demoted to Head of Traffic due to allegations of serious misconduct. This was a dramatic step, as it takes a great deal for the Dubai government to remove or demote an *asli*, or "pure" local. However, Jamman's conduct had been so egregious that they had no other option but to relieve him of his duties and demote him. The entire affair was handled very quietly, but I heard about it from one of the foreigners

34. You can read more here: man/11936981/Who-in-their-right-mind-would-want-to-visit-Dubai.html?ref=yfp.

whom he had been sponsoring in Dubai.

Like nearly every local in Dubai, Jamman also sponsored a huge number of foreigners and charged them extortionate rates. Jamman had a sort of public relations assistant named Mohamed Abraham who looked after all the various businessmen that Jamman sponsored. Abraham was a rotund local whose English was better than the average English person's, the result of being married to an Englishwoman and having lived in the UK for many years as a student. He was Jamman's right-hand man, his number-one henchman, and his partner in crime. He used his local connections and knowledge to help smooth the lives of the expat businessmen whom his boss sponsored.

Once, at a social gathering of employees of the sponsored businessmen, Abraham described—in great detail—how he handles "troublemakers," which in Dubai, mostly consists of employees asking for their rightful pay from their employers or suppliers requesting legitimate payments for goods and services. He boasted of his strategy, which was simple and superbly effective: "The moment I come across a troublemaker, I make complaint after complaint to the Dubai police in various stations all over the city."

By law, Dubai police must investigate every single complaint individually and consecutively. Every time the accused arrives at the prosecution center, he is locked up for a couple of weeks at a time, depending on the nature of the complaint. This is over and above detention at the police station. A complaint such as "Shouted loudly in office" may garner six days in judicial custody. "Stared at the women in the office several times," a very serious complaint, could get the accused as much as fifteen days in detention before being produced in court. As repeated complaints are made against the targeted individual, the police must investigate and detain the person again and again before Dubai Prosecution detains them once more before producing them to the main courts.

With this focused harassment using the machinery of the police state, the individual often loses the will to fight back against the injustice. Eventually, unable to bear the strain any longer, the individual requests that his passport be returned and cancels his residence visa. As part of this process, he is forced to sign a document written in untranslated Arabic. He often doesn't know what it says, and at that point, he doesn't care. He just wants out. These foreigners then flee to their home countries as quickly as possible, often demoralized, dejected, penniless, jobless, and possibly with a false criminal conviction on their record, which will bar them from any potential future immigration anywhere in the world. Suppliers are also forced to write off the money due, which in turn could lead to the collapse of the business itself.

It was indeed a brilliant and effective Dubai strategy to deal with so-called "troublemakers." The strategy is also known as 'perversion of the course of justice' and 'gross miscarriage of justice' in most other parts of the civilised world.

This is what happened to Lalit Mishra, a former colleague of mine. He worked for Brasstacks Trading(name changed), LLP, who were dealers in Brazilian timber. The company was owned by P.C. Bhalani, an individual of Indian origin who was sponsored by Brigadier Gamma Jamman. As a result of this chain of connections, which is what *wasta* is all about, Mohamed Abraham was entrusted with looking after the needs of the firm.

Mishra was not receiving his salary and other contractual payments on time and in full. Despite being warned not to make waves, he continued to pester his employer for his fair payment. One night, the CID picked up Mishra from his apartment in Karama, and he was immediately taken to the nearest police station. He was subsequently jailed for nine months and then deported.

Mishra was a polite, professional young man, an accountant who was always pleasant and courteous. When he suddenly disappeared from Dubai, everyone who knew him began making subtle inquiries into his whereabouts. You have to be very low-key when you are asking questions of this nature in Dubai, otherwise you could face charges yourself.

Soon, the Dubai Asian community began pressing Mishra's employer, Bhalani, for more information. Bhalani finally came out and claimed that one day, Mishra had stopped a Western expat lady who was jogging along the road and tried to kiss her. She immediately called her local boyfriend, a senior officer in the Immigration Department. He in turn called the police, and the rest, as they say, is history.

However, this story left Mishra's friends with even more questions. Who exactly was this senior officer in the Immigration Department? Who was this unknown woman? Why would a polite, gentle person like Mishra suddenly try to kiss a Western expat—and a total stranger, at that—very well knowing the consequences of such an action in Dubai?

In the end, Mishra's friends simply had to accept that this was life in Dubai. They eventually did hear from him: he was back in India and attempting to immigrate to Australia or Canada. However, thanks to his trumped-up charges, subsequent malicious prosecution, and unsafe and inhumane incarceration in Dubai, this seemed highly unlikely. His case was certainly not unusual or isolated.

Despite the strong police state infrastructure, which assumes every foreigner is guilty until proven innocent, law enforcement agencies exhibit a surprising lack of interest in and actual apathy toward genuine criminal cases. Once criminals make a getaway from Dubai—a feat that is actually quite easy and common— that's it. Case closed. It is considered impossible to bring the criminals back to Dubai to face justice, even though Dubai has the maximum number of Interpol red alerts out at any time. Ironically, most of these relate to frivolous crimes, and the big fish always get away.

One example of this is the famous Karama murder case of the early 1990s. Meenakshi Patel of India, age thirty-eight, and her husband both worked for local banks in Dubai. They lived in Karama, Pur Dubai, along with their two children, Mr. Patel's mother, and a male servant from India. At first glance, they were a normal, hard-working Dubai couple with close family ties and a good bond between the generations. But there was a dark side to the younger Ms. Patel's life that was known to few. Despite working full-time in a bank, she made frequent trips to

Mumbai, telling her work colleagues that she was going to take care of her ailing parents.

No one thought to verify this—after all, Ms. Patel was indeed close to her family. In addition, no one seemed to notice or wonder how she, a cashier in a bank with a salary of Dhs2000 per month, could have over Dhs250,000 in her personal account. In reality, Ms. Patel was a diamond courier, smuggling (or, as it is known in Dubai, re-exporting—there is no smuggling in Dubai's free-trade environment) uncut diamonds into India. This was a lucrative trade, as at the time, India had a very prohibitive customs duty on such luxury items.

Obviously, such activities cannot be done alone; she had business partners and contacts in Mumbai's underworld. Eventually, as so often happens in any such operation, Ms. Patel's greed got the better of her, and she shortchanged the gang on one particular diamond shipment.

There is a saying in Dubai that, in the underworld, trust, honesty and integrity are far more important than in normal society. This is apparently true everywhere, including in Mumbai. Ms. Patel betrayed the trust of a powerful and violent group, and now her underworld colleagues had to take their revenge and their pound of flesh.

Several members of the gang (the precise number was never known) traveled to Dubai and broke into the Patels' flat during the day while the couple were at work and the children were at school. They battered the grandmother to death with a cricket bat and held the domestic help captive, then relaxed with some tea and snacks to ease the stress of their journey from India.

As the rest of the Patels' started to return home, each child and parent were held down and systematically battered to death with cricket bats. The underworld had dished its justice.

The job done, the gang members returned to India with the male help in tow; he survived the butchery only because he had had nothing to do with Mrs. Patel's treachery. They calmly flew out of Dubai that night and soon vanished into thin air back in India. The gang did release the male help once they were safely back in Mumbai, and it is said that they even paid for a lawyer to represent him when the Indian authorities arrested him on the suspicion that he was in fact responsible for his employers' deaths.

The Dubai police initially made a great deal of noise about the case. The authorities put a curfew in place for a time, and the international press was heavily censored, so as not to give Dubai a bad name. As a result, reporting about the case soon withered, and nothing more was ever done about it.

Twenty years later, several professional assassins traveled to Dubai, thoroughly researched the area, and in a meticulously planned operation, assassinated a visiting Palestinian politician. They were able to coolly leave the country well before the Dubai police could even figure out what was going on. After the killers escaped, the Chief of Dubai Police, General Dahi Khalfan, the same person who had been the police chief at the time of the Patel murder case, made a number of grand procouncements, such as, "We know who did this. It was the Israeli Special Forces. It was directed by Mossad and backed by British Mercenaries," etc. Ultimately, it was all talk and no action. The culprits did what they did, then fled Dubai and disappeared into the great unknown.

Furthermore, even if a criminal wanted in other parts of the world remained in Dubai, so long as he or she pays their local sponsorship fees and their rent for an apartment and business offices and met other financial obligations, they are more than welcome in Dubai. What they may have done in the UK, the United States, China, India, Germany, or elsewhere does not matter. What matters is that they have the cash and have not created any trouble in Dubai itself. However, the second that person runs out of money, it is an entirely different and very serious matter. This state of affairs has given a big boost to the many white-collar criminals who make Dubai their base of operations, despite Dubai being a police state.

An example of this can be seen when a man called Shamsul joined one of the local banks as a senior trade relationship officer. I heard about him through various interviews with friends. Shamsul came across as a nice, pleasant, bespectacled man who was always helpful to his colleagues. He quickly gained a reputation as one of the most reliable employees at the bank. That is, until one day when the local police came to the bank branch to discuss a recent complaint against him, lodged by the husband of his colleague, Elina.

Shamsul had indecently propositioned Elina in the office canteen. When she refused his advances, he stole her ID from her desk and used the photograph to put an ad in the local newspaper's matrimonial column under the "Seeking Bridegroom" column, providing her home phone number. The family was soon flooded with calls from eager bachelors who were very keen to meet an attractive woman like Elina with a view toward a potential long-term relationship. It was then that her husband went to the police.

When the police came to the bank to talk to Shamsul and bank branch manager, the HR team discovered that there was no background information or outside references in Shamsul's personnel file. They quickly contacted his previous employer, a bank in Sri Lanka. The bank in Sri Lanka immediately gave them a comprehensive statement about Shamsul's track record there.

He had been a dynamic performer in India and had been posted overseas to Colombo, Sri Lanka, in recognition of his excellent performance in India. However, at the bank in Sri Lanka, over a holiday, Shamsul had transferred significant funds from corporate accounts to various ghost accounts overseas. He made plans to soon leave the country, but he was not fast enough.

When the bank reopened after the holiday, the unusual transactions were immediately spotted, and the auditors were called in. They quickly realized the scale of the crime and called the police. Shamsul was sentenced to seven years' hard labor and, after serving his sentence, was deported back to India.

Unfortunately, before the bank or the police in Dubai could act, Shamsul had vanished again. He later reappeared in Abu Dhabi, flourishing as an accounts officer with another unsuspecting employer. What Sri Lanka, a much larger and a far poorer country, could achieve, the UAE could not, despite being a police state with far more resources at its disposal. Many Shamsuls from all over the world make Dubai their home for this very reason and freely wheel and deal in businesses there.

Another recent example involves Layla De Cruz and her mother, Diane Moorcroft. Ms. De Cruz was a British model based in Dubai, and she and her mother planned and executed a truly sophisticated and innovative property scam. The two women conned a bank in England into transferring £1.5 million to a bank in Dubai by having Ms. Moorcroft pose as the millionaire owner of a vacant estate in England that was up for sale at the time. The pair convinced the bank to give them a bridge loan for the house before the house's purchasers finalized the deal.

By the time the Land Registry Department in the UK raised the alarm, it was already too late: Ms. De Cruz and her mother had already cleaned out the bank account, withdrawing the funds in cash in Dubai with ease. Of course, had there been a complaint against Ms. De Cruz by a local woman for showing off her belly button in a shopping mall or being "scantily clad at a public beach," the Dubai police would have unleashed hell on her. But in this case, they didn't see it as a problem.[35]

Yet another instance of this can be seen when Barun Singh (name changed), a senior manager at Dubai Duty-Free, wanted to sell his BMW. He told me how he had advertised that it was for sale in the local newspaper, and three men responded to

---

35. You can read the full story here: www.dailymail.co.uk/news/
article-4125734/Model-mother-face-jail-launching-1-2m-fraud.html.

the ad. They said that they wanted to test-drive the car before making an offer, and Singh, lulled by the relative security of Dubai, blithely handed over the keys. That was the last time he saw his BMW. When the men did not return, he went to the police, but they said they could not do anything about it, because in all probability, the criminals had already driven the car across the border into Oman.

At the same time, the UAE's government has been on high alert regarding social-media use ever since the Arab Spring Revolutions in 2011, which were entirely orchestrated through social media. Since that time, it has monitored social media use carefully and put a number of harsh cyber-control laws in place.

For example, in August 2016, when an Emirates Airlines Boeing crash-landed in Dubai with three hundred passengers onboard and burst into flames, people who had witnessed it immediately began talking about it on social media. The UAE government stepped in and tweeted: "#GCAA warns all residence [sic] in the #UAE to stop abusing social networks by publishing videos, news or pictures of aviation's accidents." It went on to add: "Sharing such practices is considered to be irresponsible and disrespectful to the victims, and is punishable under #UAE law." Breach of this order could lead to imprisonment.[36]

American helicopter pilot Ryan Pate did not give a second thought to moaning about his Abu Dhabi-based employers, Global Aerospace Logistics, on Facebook while

---

36. Read the full story here: http://whatson.ae/dubai/2016/08/uae-residents-warned-posting/.

he was on leave in Florida. When he returned to Abu Dhabi to resign from the firm, he was summoned to the local police station, where they confronted him with a hardcopy of his Facebook posts.[37]

In January 2018, British man Yaseen Killick, an estate agent in Dubai, went through a harrowing experience for an angry WhatsApp rant to a car dealer who had ripped him off. Killick and his wife bought a car that literally broke down within hours of the purchase. He later checked an online database and found that he had been sold a car that had been written off as totalled. He sent an angry message to the dealer, asking, "How do you sleep at night?"

He thought that was end of it, but when the couple were trying to fly to London for Christmas, they were detained, and Yaseen was taken into custody. He spent three weeks in prison before being released, all because of his angry WhatsApp message.[38]

In August 2016, Scott Richards, a forty-two-year-old dual citizen of the UK and Australia, was arrested and charged with illegal fundraising for having promoted a children's charity on his Facebook page. The crowd-funding campaign for children at the Chahari Qambar refugee camp on the outskirts of Kabul, Afghanistan, was seeking $35,000 for "new tarpaulins, blankets,

---

37. Read the full story here: www.bbc.co.uk/news/technology-31692914.

38. You can read the full story here: www.msn.com/en-gb/news/uknews/ brit-jailed-in-dubai-for-sending-angry-whatsapp-message-to-car-dealer-who-ripped-him-off/ar-BBIb4Gs?li=BBoPW.

warm clothes and socks, and sleeping bags." Richards was held in custody for twenty-two days, causing extreme distress to his wife and family. In Dubai, it is illegal to do any kind of fundraising without explicit written permission from the government.[39]

Even locals are not immune to punishments if they have committed the "serious crime" of misusing social media. In March 2017, the prominent economist, academic, and human-rights defender, Dr. Nasser bin Ghaith, a UAE citizen, was sentenced to ten years in prison for his Tweets criticizing the Emirati government.[40]

In a similar case, prominent Emirati human-rights defender and blogger, Ahmed Mansoor, was arrested in April 2016 for "using social media to defame the UAE." Even though the authorities claim he is being held at Central Prison, his exact place of detention remains unverified. He has not been allowed access to a lawyer and has been detained in solitary confinement since his arrest.[41]

Beyond social media, Dubai's government closely controls the internet within their domain. For example, a British

---

39. You can read the whole story here: www.bbc.co.uk/news/world-middle-east-37114401.

40. Amnesty International has been covering this story: www.amnesty.org/en/latest/news/2017/03/uae-prominent-academic-jailed-for-10-years-over-tweets-in-outrageous-blow-to-freedom-of-expression/.

41. You can read more about this story here: https://uk.news.yahoo.com/britain-us-urged-act-dubai-000102031.html.

expatriate whom I know was recently confused when he kept coming up with no results when he was Googling his home county of Essex in the UK. It took him a while to realize that because the word "Essex" had "sex" in it, it was banned and not coming up on searches at the time.

Skype, the popular software that allows users to make voice and video calls between computers, mobile phones, and tablet devices via the internet, has been blocked in the UAE since January 2018. According to UAE-based telecom companies Etisalat and DU, "Access to the Skype app is blocked since it is providing unlicensed Voice over Internet Protocol (VoIP) Service, which falls under the classification of prohibited content, as per the United Arab Emirates' Regulatory Framework." In addition, new laws have banned the use of Virtual Private Networks (VPN), which include Skype services.[42] Violating these laws could lead to fines between US $136,000 and US$545,000.

The United Arab Emirates' intelligence service is also actively creating an "elite task force" of cyber-security experts from around the world to help them develop a surveillance system that can be used to spy on any civilian in Abu Dhabi and Dubai. When it is complete, the government will have even more ways to tracks its citizens and foreign residents than ever before. Individuals will be monitored from the moment they leave their doorstep in the morning, to the moment they return to it at night. Their work, social habits, and behavioural patterns will

---

42. You can read the full story here: http://whatson.ae/dubai/2016/08/the-uae-government-clears-up-vpn-use-questions/.

be recorded, analysed, and archived. It may sound like science fiction, but the UAE is trying to make it a reality.[43]

Of course, the police state in Dubai can also operate much more subtly. For example, residents were recently sent a "Happiness Index Questionnaire" by the Dubai police, allegedly to help them understand why residents were dissatisfied with anything in Dubai. Within the expat community, it was rumoured that any expatriates who seemed unhappy about their life in Dubai without a valid personal reason would be referred to the Dubai prosecution.[44]

The moral of these stories is that the rule of law in Dubai mostly involves keeping Rolexes' and Mercedeses' safe. Things like human dignity, freedom of expression, and fair play for all should also have their rightful place in any society that boasts about its safety via rule of law, but that is simply not the case here.

---

43. You can read the details in the International Business Times here: https://uk.news.yahoo.com/uae-recruiting-elite-task-force-140131025.html.

44. Yahoo News originally reported this story, but it has since been taken down.

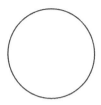

LIFE AND LIFESTYLE IN DUBAI

Dubai is known for its lavish–to the point of decadence—lifestyle. A tourist in Dubai is likely to be awestruck by its super-fast luxury cars, its glittering shopping malls (Emirates Shopping Mall is believed to be the largest in the world, though Minnesota's Mall of America might not agree), its numerous five- and six-star hotels (it is also home to the only seven-star hotel in the world, the super-deluxe Burj al Arab), the tallest building in the world (the Burj Khalifa, standing at a majestic height of 828 meters), and its numerous other deluxe residential highrise apartment buildings. Plus, there are countless super-spas and superb restaurants serving various international cuisines.[45]

---

45. Websites like whatson.ae/dubai/ or www.timeoutdubai.com/ provide information and guidance on how to plan a proper weekend.

Westerners in particular reportedly enjoy unlimited champagne brunches in Dubai's glittering hotels. Top-quality champagnes like Dom Perignon are freely available in such places.

Excellent fresh seafood is available in Dubai year-round. Restaurants like the Sea Food Market at the La Meridien on Dubai Airport Road are on par with any top seafood restaurant anywhere in the world.

The revolving restaurant Al Dawaar in the Hyatt Regency offers amazing buffet-style dining and some of the best views of Dubai. However, there isn't much to see during the lunch hour due to the fierce sun reflecting off the desert and concrete landscape. At night, though, this revolving restaurant offers stunning views of the city.

You can find top-notch cuisine from all around the world in Dubai. The Sadaf Restaurant on Al Maktoum Street has probably the best lamb biriyani in the world, second only to Shiraz's biriyani in Calcutta, India. Kwality Restaurant in Par Dubai serves authentic Indian dishes, and Ravi's in Satwa makes excellent spicy kebabs, though they are often too spicy for European and American palates. Ironically, this restaurant is highly favoured by the Western expat population. The Japanese restaurant Miyako in the Hyatt Regency serves a superb teppanyaki with chilled sake. Most of the bigger hotels offer excellent Chinese cuisine in the in-house speciality restaurants, and the Automatic Group's Lebanese cuisine is some of the best I have ever had.

But Dubai's best-kept culinary secret and its tastiest

contribution to the world of gastronomy is its shawarma. It is Dubai's most popular street food, a slow-grilled meat, either chicken or lamb, served with fresh vegetables in a special bread as a wrap. The falafel, which is the vegetarian option, is supremely delicious as well. It is truly mouth-watering and can be found in many small stands outside along the road.

In most cases, the shawarma technician will either be from the Indian state of Kerala or some other Arab nationality. The technician's nationality and their corresponding unique recipe is what gives each shawarma stand its own flavour and taste. When money is tight, many people in Dubai get by with a shawarma dinner. Bachelors also find shawarma a very handy dish.

In addition to restaurants, there are plenty of nightclubs in Dubai where live bands play current popular music every night. Many entertainers come from the Philippines and Eastern Europe, and their sounds are equally diverse.

It's never a bad idea to let one's hair down on occasion, and Dubai's nightclubs are the perfect place to do so, but keep in mind that there are always plenty of plainclothes policemen in such places to keep an eye on what the foreigners are up to. The slightest disturbance caused by alcohol or even a hint of drug use can lead to getting caught up in Dubai's grinding legal system.

Shopping is a major pastime in Dubai. For the poorer sections of the migrant class, a trip to the shopping malls during the weekend is a welcome respite, especially during the summer months, because they can take advantage of the mall's central air-conditioning to cool down, since they generally do not have the same facilities in the labor camps they call home. For the wealthier residents and for tourists, there are countless ways to "shop 'til you drop."

When in Dubai, a visit to the Dubai Duty-Free Cigarette Outlet is a good idea if you're a smoker. It's a smoker's paradise and also a good place to pick up some quality Johnny Walker Blue Label and Black-Label Whisky at reasonable prices. For those who are more health conscious, Dubai is an excellent place to buy top-quality cashew nuts, pistachios, and mouth-watering dates at very reasonable prices, as these products are grown regionally in places like Saudi Arabia (dates) and Iran (nuts).

For those short on time, a walk through the Dubai airport and the duty-free store there is a must. In fact, if you have seen these two Dubai institutions, you have seen Dubai and what it is all about. There is another advantage to this: you will not be exposed to the harsh Dubai sun, and the central air-conditioning there is some of the most effective in the city.

If you have more time, a walk through Dubai's Gold *Souk*, or gold market, is essential. For many, you have not lived your Dubai dreams until you have purchased gold there. It is said that Dubai gold is unique, and it does indeed have a bit of whitish tinge. It is some of the purest gold on the planet—an unadulterated, twenty-four karat, recession-proof investment for volatile times. The jewellery crafted from this gold is also some of the best in the world.

For the more practical minded, Par Dubai has countless

registered outlet stores, where you can secure brilliant deals on second-hand brand-name items. In Dubai, it is common practice for local men to shower good-looking women with expensive gifts. The women then sell these unwanted gifts back to the retailers, resulting in amazing deals for others.

The Hamriya Market is Dubai's fresh produce market, and it is where families shop for fresh food at reasonable prices. The local fresh fish of choice is the hammour, and it is readily and plentifully available, along with other fresh seafood like tiger prawns and lobsters.

There is plenty to do in the UAE in addition to shopping, so long as you have sufficient cash. There are amazing, though very hot, public beaches in Ajman, Jumeirah (in Dubai), Ras Al Khaimah, Fujairah, and Korfakkan, though Western women are strongly advised not to mistake these beaches for those in Europe or the Americas, as two-piece bikinis are highly frowned upon. It is quite common for hordes of men to ogle ladies in two-piece swimsuits in an embarrassing manner. In general, it is advisable for women who wish to sunbathe or swim to join a private club that has its own private beach or as a tourist inside their hotels, where they will have considerably more freedom.

There is a very famous golf club for golfing enthusiasts, though Westerners who are used to being able to play affordably may find its membership fees high. This is because it is very expensive to maintain a perfectly green golf course in the desert. Personally, I cannot comprehend how a human being can walk around in that blazing sunshine and heat with a heavy bag full of clubs, let alone enjoy a game of leisure.

Then there are the tennis tournaments and cricket tournaments to keep sports fanatics from a variety of nationalities happily engrossed. For fans of any sports, attendees should check with the authorities regarding what sort of vocal and flag-waving support they are allowed to provide their players and national teams without falling afoul of any public order breach. After all, Dubai plainclothes policemen keep close tabs on all public events. In addition, there is a thriving underworld betting syndicate for all sporting events, and unofficial gambling dens used in complete secrecy.

Many of the emirates offer fantastic amusement parks. Dubai has a world-famous, year-round ice-skating rink—quite a feat in a city where outside temperatures can reach 53 degrees Celsius (about 127 degrees Fahrenheit) for months at a time. Multiplex cinemas show the latest Hollywood and Bollywood blockbusters.

Yet despite all of these marvels, it is curious—and important to note—that there are very few bookstores in Dubai. Given the government's emphasis on keeping its local population politically and socially quiet and complacent, it is no surprise that there are few resources for expanding the mind. In addition, there only two English-language newspapers in Dubai, the *Gulf News* and the *Khaleej Times*, and both are highly censored.

It is important to remember that many of these attractions I have mentioned are intended for and largely populated by tourists. Any all-inclusive holiday package in the emirates, which may include things like a desert safari and barbecue—possibly with a performance by an attractive Lebanese or Egyptian belly dancer thrown in as a surprise—is vastly different from the actual day-to-day life of the average foreigner who lives in Dubai. Of course, this is true of all destinations. Does a three-day trip to Madrid or New York City or Paris give one a true picture of its residents' daily lives? Of course not, so why should it be any different for Dubai?

First of all, there are very serious visa restrictions for foreigners in Dubai—even for families who have lived there for decades. As has already been mentioned, UAE residence permits used to be valid for three years, though this has been cut down to two years. The only exception is if they are employed by a Dubai government department, in which case, the traditional three years still stands.

In addition, there are constant rumors about changes to the visa process. These rumours are purposefully generated and put out by the Dubai Immigration Department to keep the expat community on its toes, remind them that this is not their country, and that they are very much at the mercy of their local Emirati masters' whims and fancies. This semi-official rumor mill will churn out updates on who can and cannot obtain a visa or resident permit, and it seems to change every month. One month, it's being said that Syrian and Indian expats are being kept out; the next, that no residence permits are being issued to Pakistanis and Palestinians; and so on and so forth.

Furthermore, it is very rare for single women to obtain residence permits on their own. In general, unless a visa is sponsored by large, global, and very well-respected business, such as HSBC, Stanchart, or Morgan Stanley, which they do when making internal international transfers, a single woman is unlikely to get a UAE residence/employment permit unless there is a powerful local supporting the application. As a result, unless they have been parachuted in by a heavyweight multinational, most professional women who work in Dubai are sponsored by either their husbands or their fathers. In fact, it is not uncommon for expat girls to grow up in Dubai, complete their high school educations there, return to their native countries— whether it be the UK, the United States, India, or Pakistan—for college or university, return to Dubai with graduate degrees and accreditation, and still only be allowed to work in Dubai if their father or husband sponsors them. I personally know a large number of women in such situations.

Based on this, one might assume that Dubai is a man's world and that men get all the jobs in Dubai. While this is true to some extent, there are also very strict restrictions based on salary as to who can bring their family to the UAE. Highly skilled English-speaking expats from places like the US and the UK, who come in as senior managers or directors, are not generally affected by these restrictions. However, many young men from the developing economies of places like India, Pakistan, the Philippines, Bangladesh, and Egypt are adversely affected by these rules. Many of these men are low-income laborers or those just above them in the social order: waiters, office assistants, sales representatives, junior accountants, storekeepers, warehouse assistants, etc. Furthermore, no one really knows what these threshold income rules are, and the goalposts seem to constantly move based on the whims and fancies of the Dubai Labour and Immigration departments.

The reality is that the men who cannot afford to sponsor their families and bring them to Dubai are effectively forced widowers. As they sweat it out in the terrible desert heat, they hope and pray that their travails amid poor treatment will not be in vain and that one day, they will have a bigger salary and will be able to sponsor their families to join them in Dubai.

Despite not allowing thousands of men to bring their families with them, Dubai proclaims to love families. At every opportunity, it tries to portray itself as a great family-friendly destination, a place where families from all over the world live together in peace and harmony. Its self-promotion often contains images of families driving to the beach or having barbecues in the park or in the desert and of children happily playing outside the family home. In these images, Dubai is a place of happiness, peace, and serenity. It is a picture-perfect place of harmony and family values, where families can enjoy a peaceful coexistence with their international neighbours in a crime-free environment.

In many ways, these images of Dubai family life are accurate, as Dubai does indeed provide a safe environment for families—provided that they are high earners with sufficient cash and no adverse life situations, such as ill health, marital discord, or potential loss of employment to name a few. Dubai offers no social safety net for life's ups and downs.

However, for the "forced bachelors" of Dubai—generally dubbed "single men"—the reality cannot be more different.

In Dubai, there are two categories of "single men": those who are genuine bachelors who are not yet married, and men who are married, but had to come to Dubai without their families.

For this first type of men, especially for those from the developing nations of Asia, their initial reactions to Dubai are often bewilderment and incredulity, especially if they are coming from a small town. To these men, the gleaming skyscrapers, glamorous hotels and restaurants, and fast luxury cars are dazzling. There is a sense of disbelief at their good fortune to live in such a land. At first, these single men do not feel any restrictions in Dubai. There are restaurants and pubs everywhere, with attractive women serving in them. There are plentiful consumer products, and fantastic shopping malls offer more products than the average emperor had in his palace a century ago. For those from South Asia, where gold is as good as a deity, the jaw-dropping Dubai Gold *Souk* boggles the mind. It is difficult to blame these men for believing that they are in paradise well before their time has come.

But over time, familiarity sets in for these men and, as they say, familiarity breeds contempt. These bachelors begin to realize that they are operating in a not-so-open a prison. The mind-numbing heat starts to take its toll. Scientists say that a lack of sunshine creates depression, but have they ever addressed what relentless sunshine, with only a few days of rain every couple of years, can do to a person's mind? These men realize that their prospects for career growth, especially if they are employed by small local or expat, family-owned businesses, are nonexistant. Boredom and ennui sets in as all of these exciting opportunities for luxury become commonplace.

Their initial awe over, these men start missing their families back home, yet they do not know when they will see them again. Labor contracts state that every two years, workers can travel back to their homelands, but job security is an important issue in the Gulf. Thanks to the constant flow of cheap labor from surrounding countries, workers worry that if they go home, someone willing to take a lower salary will immediately replace them. Many do not take advantage of this option to return home for this very reason.

The constant oversupply of labour is not just a concern for the low-skilled workforce. Even for highly skilled migrants— since countries like India are churning out millions of talented, fresh professionals—job security is not a given. Even highly skilled workers in Dubai can never rest on their laurels and think of their appointments as "jobs for life."

Even a top job in the government is extremely vulnerable for expats. Foreigners are basically hired to groom younger locals and prepare them for these roles. Then, once the local has a rudimentary knowledge of their job, the expat is let go. This happens to white-collar workers, regardless of where they are from. This is known as the Government of Dubai's Emiratisation Programme. Dubai believes they need to create at least 35 to 40 million jobs for locals in the next few decades for its local population; otherwise, there will be social unrest. Hence, the need to get highly skilled expats to train the locals and then get rid of the expats as soon as possible.

Dubai's employment market is similar to the tagline from an ad for the famous Swiss watchmaker, Patek Phillipe. In its advertisements, the firm claims that when you buy a Patek Phillipe watch, you do not own the watch itself; rather, you are looking after it for the future generations. Similarly, an expat does not have a job or a career in the Gulf; he or she holds and nurtures it until the next generation of Gulf locals are ready to take it over.[46]

Every expat in a top government, bank, or quasi-public sector job nervously awaits the day when he will get a call from the HR team, letting them know that they have been terminated. Often, expats realize that their time is up when they start getting shunted from one position to another within the same organization. For example, an expat may have been working as a Letter of Credit Officer in a medium-sized branch of a government bank for several years. But then, one day, his local manager informs him that he is being transferred to a much smaller branch. This is the expat's first warning signal that his days in Dubai are coming to an end.

Unfortunately, not having received any kind of professional development training during his years in Dubai, this expat employee's skills are no longer in sync with those of his industry back in his home country, where things have continued to move forward at a rapid pace. In essence, working in Dubai does not really prepare you for anything else afterwards.

---

46. They say a picture is worth a thousand words. Take a look at www.dmcc. ae/, which displays Dubai's most amazing new enterprises. As a case study, simply browse through it and track the changing management structures of the firm over time.

We've seen this again and again throughout Dubai's recent history. In the 1970s, they were looking for oil engineers. In the 1980s and 1990s, they were looking for bank credit officers. In the early years of the new millennium, Dubai was trying to develop its stock market and the various associated commodity exchanges, so they were hiring investment and regulatory professionals. Now, block-chain technology is the big thing in Dubai. In each case, employers brought in already skilled expats from all over the world to start these industries and train local workers in them. Once the locals pick it up, the expats are sent home without having developed their own skills in any way.

However, menial positions, such as janitors, household maids, garbage collectors, and construction labourers, and lower-paying jobs in small foreign-owned firms will always be available for foreigners, simply because no locals would ever consent to doing them. Foreign workers in these positions do not have to worry about competing with locals for these jobs; they have to worry about other, more-desperate foreigners.

For those workers who do return home on holidays every few years, especially for those from the developing world, the trip soon becomes more of a potential burden than a pleasure. These bachelors quickly come to regret ever having written home about the material glories of Dubai, as their role in their family circle often devolves into being a mule for consumer goods. Every letter from home becomes a nightmare of requests: Can you bring some soap for the neighbor? Can you buy a table-tennis racket for the son's friend? Can you get a few pieces of gold jewelry for the wife and the daughter? Your sister-in-law is getting married; can you bring some gold for her as well? The list of requests is endless, and many men start dreading their trip back home, due to their ever-expanding shopping list.

In contrast, single men and women from the West are generally not subject to such social pressures, and they often use their earnings to travel and visit some of the great destinations in the region, such as Egypt, Turkey, India, Maldives, Africa, and even the Far East. Some Westerners use their surplus cash to pay off their university loans or put down a deposit for a house either back home or even in Dubai.

Whether they choose to visit home or not, workers must find ways to cope with their lives in Dubai. In a nation where everyone looks forward to the weekend, single men are the only people who hate the weekend. They have no families to spend the weekend with, and one can only spend so much time in shopping malls or chatting with friends of the same sex.

Most individuals from the developing world and with low incomes are not fully aware of the benefits of gyms and outdoor sports—nor can they afford such things—so they spend a great deal of time huddled around the TV. This leads to weight gain, nurturing silent killers like high blood pressure and diabetes. Even worse, the food in Dubai is very high quality and nutritious. For many from Asia and Africa, food back home was not so nourishing, so they had to consume large quantities of it. In Dubai, these individuals continue to consume the local high-quality food in similar proportions. Thus, overeating combined with a sedentary lifestyle very quickly leads to the familiar "Dubai Stone" and its accompanying health problems. With no ongoing medical advice on health and well-being, many immigrants from the developing world drop dead before their ailment is even properly diagnosed.

For those from Europe and the Americas, who are already aware of the dangers of obesity, they tend to look for apartments with gym facilities from the very start. Some join beach clubs to enjoy a "sun 'n' sand lifestyle," while others try their hand at watersports to maintain an active lifestyle.

No matter what they do with their free time though, boredom does eventually tend to set in. Due to Dubai's heat, there are simply a limited number of options for getting out. As with all human beings, when boredom and ennui set in, one's moral compass becomes slightly disorientated, especially in a place like Dubai, where the pursuit of money is the primary and only aim in life. People who would never have even looked at alcohol in the past often begin drinking just to ease the boredom of the Gulf lifestyle. The anxiety caused by job insecurity adds stress to this mix, causing further changes and disruptions to a single man's lifestyle.

The stress of the Gulf lifestyle is exacerbated by another factor that affects everyone in the Gulf region: debt. Debt can be a major source of stress anywhere in the world, but it assumes even greater significance in Dubai, since falling into debt there and not being able to honour the debt commitments can and will lead to imprisonment. Once a person has a job and a residency visa in Dubai, banks often fall all over themselves to loan them money. Foreigners make use of these loans to build property back home, secure local rental property, pay for private education in international schools for their children, buy a nice car, or even live in a villa in the Jumeriah area of Dubai. These are all very natural and understandable desires and dreams; often, they are the very reason why people have left their homelands and moved to a desert. But such dreams can soon turn into nightmares if the person should lose their job or their business for any reason.

Making matters worse is the fact that the private financial system of banks are connected to the Immigration Department's computer systems. Once an employment or business visa is cancelled, the banks know about it. This can be critical when a foreigner in Dubai leaves their job to start their own business. Carried away by Dubai's tremendous entrepreneurial atmosphere, many people do this, but if they have not been keeping a close eye on their personal debts and liabilities, it can easily land them in jail and then deported immediately after their release.

Another source of stress for Dubai's single expats is the fact that there are very few single women, so opportunities for dating are almost non-existent. Many take to watching pornography simply to keep in touch with what a woman looks like. Of course, if they are caught watching porn or even transporting it, they can wind up in prison, followed by immediate deportation. However, it is very important to note that there is thriving prostitution industry in Dubai.

Ladies in this trade come from all over the world, some voluntarily and some trafficked. The very well-known shortage of single women in Dubai means that they (or their sponsors) can set their prices at whatever they want. It is ironic that while single professional women often have a hard time getting a visa to come work in Dubai's IT field, for example, sex workers have little trouble coming to Dubai, despite the fact that any sexual activity outside of marriage is against the law. These women procure their visas through high-ranking locals with a great deal of *wasta* and jobs in the Immigration, Labour, or Police Departments. There is no formal red-light district, like in Amsterdam, so these ladies operate out of a variety of hotels (not all hotels in Dubai are five stars) all over Dubai, further boosting Dubai's tourism industry. This is all done with the full knowledge of the authorities, and so long as everything is kept quiet and below the radar, they have no problem looking the other way and lining their pockets. Unfortunately, because of the way these ladies dress by virtue of their profession, they tend to stand out in a crowd and are often subject to sniggers, snide remarks, and verbal passes, especially when they are on their way back home through the Dubai International Airport.

On the flip side, with such a high ratio of men to women, it is relatively easy for the rare eligible young woman to pick a suitable partner. If a single young professional woman is lucky enough to secure a work visa in Dubai, she would truly have her pick of all the single men for miles.

Given all of this, one might think that those men who make enough money to bring their families with them to Dubai are in quite an enviable position. However, being able to afford to bring their family with them introduces a whole new set of problems due to Dubai's high cost of living.

Anish Sinha is an electronics engineer with an additional degree in marketing at the post-graduate level that secured a job with a Japanese electronics firm in the Free-Trade Zone of Jebel Ali. In a personal interview, he told me that he had not applied for the position, but the firm had head-hunted him in India due to his experience, education, and talent.

His new firm offered him a substantial raise compared to what he had been making in India, plus annual return tickets for the whole family to India, an annual bonus, paid holidays, and an end-of-term gratuity. It was a generous offer, and Sinha and his family were thrilled. Still, he had his fair share of initial doubts: the fear of the unknown and of leaving a permanent job with great potential for advancement made him hesitant at first. But the financial rewards won out, and Sinha quickly made up his mind to accept the Gulf offer.

Sinha had been married for five years at that point, and he and his wife had a child, but they were still living with his parents. As the only son, it was considered his duty to look after his parents in their old age; this is the unspoken social contract in India. It took some time to convince him, but Sinha's retired father eventually reluctantly allowed his son to finally leave the nest at the age of thirty. Though Sinha had been bringing in a fairly decent income by Indian standards, it was not enough to care for five people, especially given India's double-digit inflation. In addition, the family was incurring a great deal of medical bills, as Sinha's mother had suddenly become bed-ridden from a mysterious disease that baffled the local doctors. Thus, a large increase in salary would be a boon to the entire family.

His Japanese employers sorted out Sinha's visa and labour contract within a week of his arriving in Dubai, and he immediately applied for family residence for his wife and son. Seven days later, the family was reunited. After his wife got over the initial shock of Dubai's extreme glamor compared to their hometown of Coimbatore, they went apartment hunting.

Sinha's new colleagues warned him not to rent accommodation far from the office, or else a substantial portion of his salary would go to taxi fares. As a result, the family found a decent, two-bedroom flat with central air conditioning quite close to Jebel Ali on Sheikh Zayed Road, just off the Dubai-Abu Dhabi Highway. It was in a new building, because they had been warned that slightly older buildings—those built even five or ten years ago—often have a range of problems related to their plumbing and air conditioning.

Sinha's new colleagues had also informed him that he could get an apartment with window air conditioning units for cheaper than those with central air conditioning, but the torrid summer heat in Dubai is best handled by a central a/c unit. Global warming is affecting the Gulf region even more than other places, and Sinha decided to ensure that his family was comfortable, even though it would cost him a bit more. This was a wise decision, as they soon discovered that central air conditioning is not a luxury, but more of a necessity, in the Gulf.

Sinha and his wife were also lucky in that they found an apartment whose rental arrangements were handled by its local owner, which made everything smoother and marginally cheaper. The rental contract was for one year and was to be paid upfront in three post-dated checks. This was a very favorable term for them, as most landlords wanted the entire annual rent paid upfront in a single installment.

The local landlord, Mr. Ahmed Al Bannai, had a day job with the Dubai Immigration Office. Like most well-to-do Dubai locals, he worked at his day job until two p.m., went home, had lunch, slept for a couple of hours, and then was back up at seven p.m. to run his own business from his private offices. His steady salary from his government job and the profits from his own enterprises made Mr. Al Bannai a well-to-do, educated, and pleasant person to deal with. He had lived in the UK for several years as a paying guest with an English family and was fluent in both the language and the cultural nuances of the English-speaking world.

After many handshakes between the two men, the rental contract (written in Arabic, of course) was signed, and the post-dated checks were handed over, along with a 10 percent security deposit. With the property secured and his wife delighted, the couple and their child moved into their new apartment with central air conditioning, despite having no furnishings at all—not even mattresses to sleep on.

This was quickly remedied though, and the next few weeks were truly amazing for the family. Once Sinha's bank saw that he had a good job and a steady salary being directly deposited into the bank, they offered him a wide range of loans and credit options. With that, he and his family went out each evening to buy furnishings: curtains, carpets, beds, a refrigerator, a stove and oven, a sofa set, a TV, and a CD player. They bought clothes for themselves and school uniforms for their son. It was all exciting—the stuff of dreams.

His wife, Swati, was delighted with their purchases from top brands like Ikea, Sony, and Samsung. She was thrilled by the opportunity to finally be able to set up her own home without the interference of her in-laws. The couple's son, Rahul, was also delighted that he would now have his own bedroom—a rarity in India—and he requested some Superman and Batman posters to decorate his room. He wanted it to look like the rooms of his rich friends back home.

However, in making all these household purchases, Sinha had maxed out his fairly large credit limit. He had to take out loans to pay for his son's school fees at a semi-decent private school near their residence and to send money back to his parents in India, so they could continue his mother's medical treatments and pay off a high-interest loan they had taken out to marry off Sinha's only sister.

Sinha realized that once he took into account the credit card bill, the loan repayments, the rent, and Rahul's school fees, there was not much disposable income left. Plus, they still had to pay for the regular costs of living: things like the water bill, the electricity bill, the mobile phone bill, and, of course, food.

Still, even with all that, the family was far better off financially in Dubai than they had been in India. Sinha felt certain that within a few months, the family would have some money in their savings account; if they could live on a tight budget for a few years, they would be well on their way to affluence. His family was happy, and he was in an international assignment in a high profile city; that is all that mattered.

Of course, there were certain niggling irritations that Sinha tried to ignore and put down to cultural differences. For example, at work one day, his colleagues were discussing driver's licenses in different countries. Sinha mentioned that he had had a license from India.

The only local in the office, a man named Mohamed al Badri, laughed out loud. "Your Indian driver's license is *kachra* [dirty, useless]," he cackled. "Did you know that I can buy an Indian driver's license here in Dubai?"

At that, the rest of Sinha's colleagues burst into laughter.

Al Badri often made fun of Indians, as well as Bangladeshis and Pakistanis. He often addressed Sinha mock-lovingly as "You *kachra*, *miskin* [poor] Indian." He once proclaimed, "You Indians eat stones for dinner." Another time, he saw an order from a Bangladeshi firm for US$100,000-worth of supplies and immediately quipped, "This must be Bangladesh's biggest export order ever!"

Everyone else in the office tolerated these remarks and even laughed at them. After all, it was Badri's country, and he could afford to crack a few jokes at the expense of foreigners. As a result, Sinha kept his head down, ignored all the racial banter, and just focused on his work and his family.

Soon enough, Sinha and his family started making contacts with members of the Indian community from their home state of Kerala. They were invited to gatherings with others from this group. At their first such event, Sinha enjoyed his first-ever genuine chilled Budweiser beer. His family enjoyed their Cokes and lemonades, along with a sumptuous fish curry—the fish having been imported all the way from their native state in India.

His wife, Swati, learned that there were fifteen families in this community, and they took turns throwing such parties each quarter. That way, they evenly distributed the hard work and costs of such events, and everyone could enjoy a good party. This group also made occasional visits to the shopping malls together, especially during sales. There was also the occasional weekend trips to the beaches in other emirates. Of course, all of these things cost money, but Sinha was simply glad that his family was connected to the community.

But things kept coming up: his son wanted to have a birthday party at McDonald's with a few classmates, something he could never even dream of doing back in India. His wife dreamed of buying some gold jewellery for herself for Diwali, the Hindu Festival of Lights. Back in India, all they could afford for her during that time of year were a few new saris. Sinha was happy that he could provide these luxuries for his family for the first time. The family had already started to feel economically well off.

Then, one day, when Sinha got home from work, the *nathur* (the building's caretaker) approached him in the lobby and handed him a letter in a brown envelope. It was written entirely in Arabic, and Sinha could not make heads or tails of it, so he asked the *nathur* what it was all about

The *nathur*—a fellow Indian from Coimbatore who had been

living and working in Dubai for twenty years and could read Arabic—told him that someone from the Dubai government had dropped off letters for all of the building's residents. The municipality had just instated a 5 percent *shulka*, or tax, to be paid every time a rental contract is signed or renewed.

Sinha had been under the impression that Dubai was completely tax-free, so the next day, he queried the landlord's office, thinking that perhaps the *nathur* had misunderstood. The manager explained that this had nothing to do with the landlord, but was instead a mandatory new tax the Dubai government had imposed to offset the revenue lost from falling oil prices. Since 2014, Dubai has progressively eliminated subsidies on electricity, water, and gas to help offset these losses. Now, they were moving to impose new taxes on those who do not own property. For Sinha, this meant an increase in his cost of living without an increase in his salary. *Not good*, he thought.

But apart from the money itself, he was taken aback by the way this new *shulka* had been introduced by the government. There was no discussion, no debate, no public hearings, no consultations, and no advance warning. It was simply, "Pay this, or else!" Even the actual notification was in a language that more than 70 percent of Dubai's population does not read.

Still, Sinha tried to console himself. After all, taxes are a natural part of life. There is no such thing as a free lunch, and who ever said that life was fair? After all, the city of Dubai kept the streets very clean and in good repair.

As the family was coming up on the end of their first year in Dubai, they were excitedly preparing for their first trip back home. They constantly went shopping, looking for items for their friends and families back home.

It was at this point that the *nathur* once again approached Sinha with an envelope after work one day. The *nathur* explained that it was the new rental contract for the coming year. When Sinha examined it, he realized that the rent had gone up by 20 percent, meaning that, when coupled with the new Dubai municipality rental tax, the family's monthly rent had gone up by 25 percent.

To make matters worse, the *nathur* then added that since there was a heavy demand for apartments in the area, the owner would no longer accept the rent in three post-dated checks. Henceforth, the rent had to be paid entirely upfront in one check. If the tenants were not willing to accept the new terms, they were expected to leave the property seven days before the end date of their rental contract so that new tenants could move in. No discussions.

A 25 percent increase in rent, plus having to pay for it upfront would mean having to borrow more money from the bank, as the family did not have that level of financial reserves yet. The couple discussed the increase in rent and their options over the next few sleepless nights.

Moving was an option, but to where? To an older building, which might have problems or lack central air conditioning? To a building further from Sinha's office, which would increase his commute time and cost? In addition, moving is a big hassle in Dubai, and relocation costs are high. Plus, if the family moved, everything they had spent on the beautiful carpets and curtains would have to be written off, since they couldn't be refitted for the new apartment. They decided to stay and simply borrow the money to pay the enhanced rent upfront.

Soon after, Rahul brought a sealed envelope home from school addressed to his parents. Sinha and his wife couldn't believe their eyes when they opened it: the school fees would be 25 percent higher for the next term, and, just like the rent, everything would have to be paid up front all at once.

Well, education is education, Sinha reasoned. After all, when he had been a child back in India, his own parents had said, "Even if we must starve, we have to ensure that the children's education continues." There was no risk of the family starving, and at least the school had notified them early. When he met with the bank's loan officer, Sinha simply asked for a larger loan to cover both the rent and Rahul's school fees.

The family made some sacrifices to make their new finances cover everything. They decided to skip going to India for vacation that year, resolving to go the next year instead. Sinha cancelled his plans to take driving lessons, which would enable him to get a driver's license.

In addition, they sublet one of the two bedrooms to two single Indian women who were nurses in a nearby state hospital. Unfortunately, with this, what had once been a peaceful, pleasant home quickly became crowded and hellish. Swati had trouble getting along with one of the women, and they constantly clashed over the use of the kitchen and its cleanliness.

At the end of the second year, when the *nathur* delivered a rental contract for the coming year that showed another 20 percent increase in rent and Rahul brought home another letter stating that his school fees had similarly increased another 20 percent, the couple decided that enough was enough. They gave notice to their sub-tenants, wrote off their beloved carpets and curtains, and moved to Sharjah.

Unfortunately, their Dubai landlord refused to return their original security deposit on the flimsy grounds that they had hammered two nails into the walls to put up family photos. Sinha was angry, but knew there was nothing he could do about it unless he wanted to involve the courts and the police—a risky and pointless exercise.

Though Sinha's commute time and costs increased considerably, and their weekend jaunts to Dubai shopping malls came to a halt, they had some relief from the high Dubai rents and school fees. The Sharjah municipality taxes were also marginally lower at 4 percent. They felt that this was a wise move, as the rent in Dubai was simply destroying any dreams of financial security they had.

But, when at the end of year three, the *nathur* of their new building in Sharjah delivered a rental contract with a 20 percent increase, and Rahul's school fees were raised as well, it was the straw that broke the proverbial camel's back. The husband and wife decided that Sinha would remain in Dubai as a "forced bachelor" in a shared accommodation, while Swati and Rahul would return to India. It was the only way that their so-called tax-free income would not be eaten up by rent and a vastly overpriced education system.

This family had come to Dubai with great hopes of living a

comfortable, safe, and high quality life. Unfortunately, no one forewarned them that the expensive rental market and high cost of living could negatively impact their lifestyle over time.

This story is about a family from India, but sadly, it is an oft-repeated and familiar story across all segments of the expatriate population in Dubai, whether they are from the East or the West. In addition, as of this writing in early 2018, the international media is reporting that the UAE is introducing 5 percent value-added tax on some goods and services.[47] In light of this, it is important to wonder whether personal taxes for foreigners are coming as well. Could this be the beginning of the end of tax-free living for expats?

There is a saying in the United Kingdom that if the US sneezes, the UK catches pneumonia, implying the influence the US has over the UK economy. It is very similar in the Persian Gulf. There, "Big Brother" Saudi Arabia leads the way for the other six Gulf nations, and that country's actions are generally a harbinger of what is to come for the rest. As of 2018, Saudi Arabia is planning to tax all foreigners and remove all foreign

---

47. You can read more about this here: https://government.ae/ en/information-and-services/finance-and-investment/taxation/ valueaddedtaxvat.

workers from the public sector within the next three years.[48] Changes are coming to the Gulf region, and all foreigners contemplating moving there need to be aware of this fact.

---

48. You can read more about this at: https://uk.finance.yahoo.com/video/ saudi-arabia-considers-tax-expat-050813379.html, https://www.thenational. ae/business/economy/saudi-arabia-increases-salaries-and-allowances-to- offset-vat-impact-1.693110, and https://stepfeed.com/saudi-arabia-s-public- sector-will-fire-all-expat-workers-within-3-years-9052.

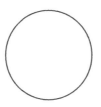

THE SOCIAL HIERARCHY IN DUBAI: SOCIETY'S PECKING ORDER

Those of us who cringe at and complain about racial discrimination in the West should have a look at Dubai's social structure some time, where this kind of discrimination is common, openly practiced, and widely accepted as a way of life. In short, there are different rules for expats from different countries and of different ethnicities.

Roughly speaking, this is Dubai's social pecking order:

1. **Local locals**: These are the Bedouins, the original inhabitants of this land. They are considered *asli*, or "pure," locals and command the highest rank in the pecking order. They are the most powerful people in

Dubai society, and the government and police always think twice before messing with them. They often come with names like "Obaid" or "Juma," with the word "Al" between the first and second name, and they can be recognized by their local dress and the traditional Emirati headgear, the *disdash*. Generally speaking, they have darker skin, due to their being descended from roaming nomads from the African continent. They speak the local Arabic dialect and just enough Hindi or Urdu and English to get by. Many still live in the desert and are in the traditional business of breeding camels for racing. This is a very lucrative profession, as camel racing is quite popular among the wealthy. Camel breeders in Dubai are somewhat similar to racehorse breeders in the West, in that they cater to the needs, wishes, and whims of the wealthy. As a result, their bank balances are very healthy indeed.

2. **Iranian Locals:** These are the current elite of Dubai society, as they own nearly all of the big local businesses. They are the descendants of Iranians who came to Dubai fifty or sixty years ago—and maybe even earlier—for trading purposes when Dubai was more of a desert than even a fishing village. They were and are essentially traders, ferrying goods between Dubai and neighboring countries like Saudi Arabia, Iran, and Yemen. As Dubai grew and the oil boom came in the early 1970s, they took advantage of this and transformed their small-time operations into multi-billion-dollar businesses. They

somehow secured UAE nationality—a rarity, since this is almost never given to foreigners—during this period and bought or were awarded large tracks of land in the desert, on which they built residential properties and shopping malls and laid the foundation for modern Dubai.

They possess names like "Yousuf" or "Khoury" and lack the "Al" in the middle of their names that the local locals have. They also have fairer skin and sharper facial features than the local locals. They generally wear the local dress because they understand that it is the power apparel in the Gulf, which will get them respect, awe, and admiration from the foreign community and will help keep them out of any controversy within the local community.

This point about apparel is an important one. If a man in New York or London or Hong Kong wears a smart suit, he is making a fashion statement, telling the world something about who he is as a person, such as his personal tastes and his position in the business world. But in the Gulf, the *kandura* is a different matter. It is a statement of national power, not just personal fashion. Wearing it displays the nation's importance to others; here, the wealthy and powerful do not capitulate to Western fashion norms. In their land, their norms rule. Even if a local man loves to wear jeans, for example, he will not do so publicly in Dubai, due to the fear of not being respected as a local. He will wear his jeans in

London or New York or Munich or Rio, but never at home.

3. **Locals of Indian, Pakistani, or Yemeni Origin**: These individuals are of South Asian origin, but they wear the local dress, the *kandura*. It is not uncommon for wealthy and even not-so-wealthy locals to marry Indian, Yemeni, and Pakistani women, and these locals are the offspring of such marriages. They speak fluent Hindi or Urdu or Arabic and watch Bollywood films, but they maintain their distance from the South Asian expat community unless they are sponsoring Asian businesses and businessmen.

4. **White British and American Expats:** This is self-explanatory. However, Americans or British citizens of other ethnic origins do not occupy such an elevated rank.

5. **Mixed-Race or Fair-Skinned Arabs:** These individuals are generally from countries like Syria and Lebanon. They speak Arabic, but also English or French, due to their nations' colonial histories. They are also more fair-skinned than many other Arabic speakers, which is important, as having fair skin is a key criteria for being well treated in Dubai outside of the "local local" category. In fact, there is a keen contest between groups 4 and 5 regarding their pecking order in Dubai society.

6. **Arab Nationals from Egypt and Jordan:** These individuals are fellow Arabic-speakers, but tend to not be as fair-skinned, thus they fall slightly lower in the

pecking order.

7. **Palestinians, Moroccans, and Algerians—The "Other" Arab Nationals:** These groups are somewhat more marginalized than other Arab nationals. In the case of Moroccans and Algerians, there simply are not that many of them in Dubai. Their national communities are smaller, have fewer connections, and thus, have less *wasta*. After the Arab Spring, which took off in several North African nations, the UAE introduced stricter visa rules for citizens of those nations, for fear that they will stir up popular resentment. In the case of Palestinians, they do not have a "proper" country of their own, so they are looked down on as being weak.

8. **Everyone Else**: This category encompasses all other nationalities and ethnicities. If someone is a citizen of the UK or the US and speaks with a British or American accent but belongs to an ethnicity not included in any of the above categories, they will be treated like anyone else in Group 8. There are strong internal tensions within this category, with various nationalities and ethnicities claiming superiority over others. Some believe they are superior because they primarily supply bankers and other white-collar workers to the UAE and look down on the groups that primarily supply the manpower for menial jobs.

All of this said, keep in mind that, like all things in Dubai, social structures are fluid and flexible. For example, at the moment, the UAE is not very keen to take in Syrians anymore, despite their fairer skin. The Syrian Civil War is displacing a number of people, and the UAE does not want poor, troublesome refugees—it wants businessmen with cash to spare. Thus, the UAE is currently claiming that because it is a small country, it cannot handle a large influx of a foreign population. In addition, in Dubai, money is the most important thing that determines one's standing. Yes, most Indians and Pakistanis are treated very poorly, but if an Indian person has sufficient cash to flash around, he can very quickly ascend the social staircase, as long as his money lasts.

The beauty of this system is that all foreigners know their exact social standing within a few days of arriving in Dubai. Whether it is the bus driver from Manchester, the computer programmer from India, the shop assistant from Sri Lanka, the waiter from Eastern Europe, or the businessman from China, everyone in Dubai fits into a precise box based on their color, profession, religion, and language. By ticking these social indicator boxes, everyone knows precisely where they fit into this society, how they should behave, and what they can expect from others.

And when push comes to shove, it is definitely better to be at the top end of the pecking order. In early 2018, British journalist Francis Matthew was sentenced to only ten years in prison in Dubai for murdering his wife. Normally, this sort of crime merits the death penalty in the Gulf region. By UAE standards, ten years in prison is very lenient indeed, and many believe Mr. Matthew's status as a white British national played a large part in his comparably light sentence.[49]

Although the UAE is keen to promote itself to the rest of the world as the picture of social cohesion—a social melting pot with everyone living together in harmony—this is not necessarily the case. Each of these groups lives a very tightly compartmentalized life, only socializing within their own communities. All Indians do not mix with all other Indians. But it is safe to say that well-educated professionals from the city of Kolkatta will mix with other well-educated professionals from Kolkatta. Even if an Indian family, Palestinian family, and a Filipino family have all been next-door neighbours in the same building for several years, it would not be surprising to learn that not only do they not know each others' names, they may not have even ever said hello to each other in all these years.

All expatriates, whether Filipino, Indian, English, Iranian, African, or American, have one thing in common: they do not want anything to do with the local population, and the feeling is mutual. A person might live in Dubai for twenty years and never once have been invited to dinner at a local colleague's house or to attend a local marriage ceremony.[50]

It is very much an "us versus them" society, with locals on one side and expats on the other. It is no wonder that expats

49. You can read more about this case here: www.msn.com/en-gb/news/ uknews/british-newspaper-editor-francis-matthew-jailed-in-dubai-for- beating-his-wife-to-death-with-a-hammer/ar-BBKETT.
50. You can read more about this phenomenon here: www.telegraph.co.uk/ expat/life/living-in-dubai-why-dont-expats-integrate-with-emiratis/.

throughout the whole region were delighted when Saddam Hussein occupied Kuwait in the early 1990s: the Kuwaitis were considered the richest and the rudest of the Gulf locals. Every expat in the region was confident that Hussein would teach "those rude brats" a lesson or two in manners.

During the Kuwaiti occupation, the expat community in the region went into overdrive with their crude and, at times, racial jokes. Of course, these jokes were only told in private as a form of protest against the repression in the Gulf; it is the only form of protest that the average expat can ever dream of. These jokes might be considered politically incorrect today, but I include them here to make it clear what was going within the Gulf expat community at the time. The author of this book in no way condones any form of racial or gender profiling.

One such joke was based on the fact that it is common for Sri Lankan women to serve as household help in the region. Once Hussein occupied Kuwait, and Kuwaitis became refugees (special refugees though, as most of the five-star hotels in Dubai were requisitioned by the exiled Kuwaiti government to accommodate their displaced people), the expat community joked, "Let's place an ad in the local paper: 'Sri Lankan family looking for a Kuwaiti helper.'"

Another joke that made the rounds at the time was, "Why did the Kuwaiti soldiers surrender so quickly? Because they were looking for Indians, Pakistanis, and Sri Lankans to carry their rifles for them, but they couldn't find any, so they decided not to fight."

Finally, there was the joke about the Emir of Kuwait running off to the safety of regional Big Brother, Saudi Arabia. The next morning, when he woke up, he found the entire Kuwaiti army outside his temporary palace. Surprised and angry, he rebuked them: "Soldiers, why are you here? You should be on the battlefield fighting Saddam!" The Kuwaiti soldiers sheepishly replied, "We really love you King, and followed you all the way here, just to be near to Your Highness. We can fight some other time."

In reality, social integration is not one of Dubai's primary aims. In fact, it regards such silly notions as bad, since it could potentially give foreigners the idea that they are welcome to settle there. The country treats its foreign workers as a temporary necessary evil that are there to get the country to the next level and then it is *Masalam(Bye) Sukran(Thanks) Habibi(Dear).*

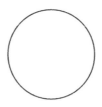

DUBAI AND THE DRIVER'S LICENSE

Dubai does not yet have a world-renowned university like Oxford, Cambridge, or Harvard. Several Western universities are adding campuses or branches in Dubai and Abu Dhabi, but foreigners are not exactly rushing to Dubai just to study. There are no large foreign student populations like they have in the UK or the US. Foreigners come to Dubai to see the world's tallest buildings, to shop for designer brands in the world's biggest shopping malls, and to make some quick money if they can; they do not come for study and wisdom.

But there is one essential qualification needed to survive and thrive in Dubai, regardless of what qualifications an expat holds from their native countries: the world-famous Dubai driver's license. It is Dubai's 'O'-levels, 'A'-levels, graduate, postgraduate, and doctoral program all rolled into one. It is the ultimate must-have for any Dubai resident. One's job, business, and quality of family and social life are completely determined by the possession of a coveted Dubai driver's license. It is also the first step to climbing Dubai's social ladder.

Dubai is a car-proud city, and size really does matter there when it comes to anything on four wheels. The make, model, and license plate number of your car determine your social standing. Recently, a foreign businessman paid several million U.S. dollars to purchase a coveted Dubai license plate in an auction to prove that he had made it in Dubai and could hobnob with the locals–a great honor for an expat. But, if he doesn't have a driver's license, he still has no car. Simply put, the possession of a driver's license separates the "haves" from the "have nots" in Dubai.

More than that though, having a driver's license in Dubai is not a luxury—it is a sheer necessity. Taxis are expensive for the average wage-earner and thus can cut into the cost of living. Simply put, having a driver's license reduces the cost of living.

Also, since it is an important qualification, the driver's license can open new doors for lucrative professional opportunities. For all marketing jobs, a valid UAE license is a mandatory requirement, as these individuals must frequently travel between the various emirates. In addition, as rents rise in Dubai, a driver's license permits people to move to nearby Sharjah or Ajman while still holding down their job in Dubai.

Having a driver's license can also open up opportunities for leisure. It allows families to drive to the shopping mall or to the beach for the weekend. If even one member of a close-knit group gets hold of a license, it is a great boon to all, because they can catch a ride to places they never could have reached before.

Let's first look at who does *not* need a Dubai driver's license. License-holders from the UK, the USA, and thirty-four other developed nations do not need to go through the gruelling process of obtaining a driver's license in Dubai. Instead, they can simply go to the Dubai Traffic Department—a division of the Dubai Police Department—and exchange their own nation's driver's license for one of Dubai's.

In fact, a UK or US driver's license-holder is guaranteed to impress the Dubai police with the very sight of their license. These documents seem to be positively mesmerizing for the Dubai Police Department, and they always immediately issue a Dubai license to the holders of such rarified documents on the spot. Thus, a new arrival from the UK or the US with a license from their own country can, within days of arrival, jump into their brand-new, shiny 'four-wheeler' and speed off for a desert safari. Citizens of Australia, Canada, New Zealand, the European Union, and other wealthy countries like Singapore need to check the Dubai Driving License website to determine whether they fall within the exempt category.

So who *does* need to take a driving test to secure the much-coveted Dubai driver's license? The rest of the world, especially Indians, Pakistanis, Sri Lankans, Bangladeshis, and Filipinos, who comprise the bulk of Dubai's foreign population. Funnily enough, citizens of these countries find it extremely difficult to get a license in Dubai, especially if they have driven in their native countries. They are told, "You were not taught to drive properly back home. Here in Dubai, we will teach you how to drive correctly and get rid of your bad driving habits." Of course, even within these communities, people with great deal of money and/or *wasta* get their driver's licences very quickly.

So what is it about the Dubai driver's license that makes it so difficult to obtain? As with many things in Dubai, no one really knows. There are various theories or apparent explanations for the government's hesitation to hand out driver's licenses, such as the authorities' wish to control CO_2 emissions or the fact that Dubai is a small city, and if too many licenses were issued, there would be too many cars and, hence, more accidents. Some say it is to keep Dubai's roads safe and that drivers from other countries are reckless. While there are no statistics to support this, anecdotal evidence suggests that it is actually young locals who are more likely to drive recklessly than expats.

Despite this, locals never have any difficulties getting a driver's license. In fact, many local youths start driving well before they have even applied for the learner's license. It is only expats from India, Pakistan, Bangladesh, Sri Lanka, the Philippines, and other such countries who find it so amazingly difficult to get a Dubai driver's license.

The Dubai Driving Test is administered by the Dubai Police. For many foreigners, the sight of a uniformed Dubai police officer—let alone having to sit beside one in a car for an extended period of time—heightens the applicant's stress and anxiety, causing them to make mistakes they never would have normally made. Many fail for this very reason and end up having to take the test yet again.

The Dubai government recognizes that this presents a fantastic business opportunity, and it issues permits to locals to set up driving schools, such as the Emirates Driving Institute, where police officers visit the school directly to assess the students in their test. However, it will not be cheap.[51] In fact, driving lessons are a big business in Dubai, given that so many expats are so desperate to get a license. They are willing to pay almost any price for lessons that might improve their plight in Dubai. This situation is ruthlessly exploited by both the legitimate the driving schools and the somewhat less-official "driving instructors."

The driving test itself is divided into five parts, with garage, reverse, hill, theory, and road tests. Each part is more gruelling than the last, and many expat learners keep attempting and failing the final one, the road test, again and again over the years. Some become nervous wrecks over time and become distraught at the mere mention of the driving test. Even more pathetic are the cases of drivers who have driven thousands of miles in their home countries, yet keep failing the Dubai driving test. They are never given any reason why and only get back a piece of paper with a huge black cross, indicating failure.

---

51. Emirates Driving Institute provides excellent driving instructors and other training facilities, and if a learner is serious about getting their license in Dubai, it is highly advisable to attend such an elite school. To learn more about Dubai driving schools and the Dubai driver's licence, you can visit the website of the Emirates Driving Institute: www.edi-uae.com/.

There is no feedback, no guidance, no words of encouragement for these driving hopefuls, just ruthless rudeness and abject racial contempt from the policemen who give the tests. The Dubai police almost seem to get a perverse pleasure from failing foreigners who have to take the driving tests. Their facial expressions, their smirks, and even their tone of voice when handing back the failing results seem to be designed to discourage.

Sarabjit Sharma, an expat in Dubai I know very well, has taken the final road test twenty-three times at the last count. He becomes a complete nervous wreck every time he gets a new assigned date for the road test, which can be several weeks after a failed attempt. He is depressed for several days before the test, spends several hundred dirhams on driving lessons, and his family speaks of it to no one, lest he fail again from sheer nervousness. It has become a ridiculous situation and a complete embarrassment for this potential driver; yet again and again, he goes off to take his test and comes back with another huge black cross. There is no guarantee of when or even if Sharma will ever pass the test.

At the same time, as expats from most other countries undergo rigorous and at times embarrassing driving lessons and testing, it is the young local population—which often zips around the crowded city at breakneck speeds—that are involved in most of the fatal accidents in Dubai, simply because of the way they drive. Do all of the young local drivers who create a mayhem of screeching tires, high-performance cars, and racing joyrides every Thursday evening near the Satwa roundabout have an authentic UAE driving license? Are the police even brave enough to challenge these dangerous local drivers? Are there any official statistics to prove that expat drivers are the dangerous ones and thus need such rigorous training and testing? The answers to all three questions is, of course not.

In addition, recall that, at night, Dubai's streets are constantly patrolled by plainclothes CID officers and littered with speed cameras, which impose hefty speeding fines of Dhs3000/US$817/£600 per breach. In July, 2018 a British tourist racked up £36000 (yes, £36K) in speeding fines in less than four hours on 31st July ,2018 while holidaying in Dubai! If any expat driver were ever to be caught with even the slightest hint of alcohol or any other intoxicant in their system, Dubai-style justice would be served quickly and brutally, no questions asked. While I am not defending or condoning driving intoxicated, there would be no polite, "Sir, could you please step out of your car and take five steps without support?" It would be more like, "That's going to cost you five years of your life." Of course, there is no information on what would happen if an intoxicated local behind the wheel were to be apprehended.

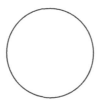

THE HEAT IN DUBAI

Dubai is a city of the desert. The government's tourism division markets Dubai as a pleasant vacation spot with year-round sunshine. It sets itself up as a place with a nice, warm climate, plenty of sunshine, fantastic shopping, great beaches, wonderful food, and amusement parks to rival Euro Disney or Disney World in Orlando—in short, a great family vacation destination along with a great entrepreneurial spirit.

Dubai aims to be a super-deluxe Spain, Malta, Italy, Monaco, Miami, Melbourne, Singapore, Las Vegas, and Panama—in fact, all of the world's greatest destinations—rolled into one. Why visit these destinations separately, when you can enjoy the benefits of them all in one place and at a fraction of the cost (really!)? Plus, it's only a stone's throw away from home for Dubai's main target clientele: the booming Asian travel markets of China and India and the traditional hub of international travel, the UK and Europe.

To be fair, Dubai does indeed enjoy 365 days of sunshine each year, as their marketing brochures promise. But they are 365 days of torturous sunshine in which the sun scorches everything it touches. After all, it *is* a desert and very humid desert at that, with occasional dusty sandstorms.

During the summer months, the average temperatures in the Gulf region are between 45 and 55 degrees Celsius (113 to 131 degrees Fahrenheit), and it can actually feel like a 60-degrees-Celsius (140-degrees-Fahrenheit) sauna. Due to Dubai's proximity to the sea, the high humidity makes the heat even more unbearable and oppressive. Between the months of May and August, the moment one steps outside an air-conditioned room, it feels like you have been wrapped in a hot towel. The heat is relentless, horrific, mind-boggling, and simply putrid. It is an all-consuming heat. A mere walk from one's apartment or office to the car park can completely drench a person in sweat. It only starts cooling down—if such an expression can even be used—very late in the evening, but because of the severe humidity, the discomfort does not go away until late at night, if it goes away at all, especially during the summer months. During midday, drivers will witness mirages–double images created by convection currents—on Dubai roads, much like in the open desert.

It is rumored that in Dubai, the exact temperature cannot even be made public, due to United Nations and International Labour Organization rules that state that if outside temperatures are above a certain threshold, human beings should not be allowed to work outdoors. If that rule were strictly followed, it is likely that very few immense concrete towers would ever get built in Dubai.

During the summer, most of Dubai's five-star hotels offer discounted, all-inclusive packages to woo travellers away from the sunshine of the French, Spanish, and Italian Rivieras. If these well-known, classy destinations are sun-kissed, then Dubai is sun-snogged at this time of the year. This is when all the locals who can afford to bail out of Dubai do so and make a beeline for cooler climates, such as London, if they have the money. If they can't afford London, Mumbai and its monsoon rains are popular. Many locals are also heading to Bosnia these days as well.

During the rest of the year, the temperatures are much more bearable, but they still cannot compare to the winter sunshine of Europe, Asia, and the Americas. Even in the relatively "cooler" months of December and January, temperatures can easily reach 35 to 40 degrees Celsius (95 to 104 degrees Fahrenheit) during midday, and lounging by the pool or at the beach all day long is not advisable from a health perspective.[52] I have listened to many people from Europe gushing about their upcoming warm-weather vacation to Dubai; upon their return

---

52. To get an even better idea of the temperatures in and around Dubai, see this MSN link, which talks about the temperatures in Kuwait in mid-July 2016. Kuwait is just a one-and-a-half hour flight from Dubai: www.msn.com/en-gb/news/weather/kuwait-swelters-in-record-breaking-54c-heat-the-highest-temperature-ever-recorded-on-earth/ar-BBuJmI4?li=BBo.

though, there is an eerie silence.

The West is slowly starting to recognize the extreme temperatures in Dubai, but the East does not have the same amount of information at its disposal, even in today's digital "Googlized" world. As a result, vacationers in India and China are frequently sold on "cheap" holiday vacation packages, completely unaware of how extreme the heat is and how that will impact their holiday.

These days, whenever someone is browsing the internet looking at anything even vaguely vacation- or travel-related, a listicle will invariably come up with a title like "The Ten Best Long-Haul Destinations in the World" or "The Ten Best Expat Destinations in the World." Dubai and/or the UAE will almost always appear in the first three slides, reminding people that it is a must-see destination and that they don't know what they are missing until they get there. This is all part of Dubai's carefully crafted digital self-marketing efforts to encourage foreigners to book a summer-discounted Dubai hotel room, jump on an Emirates Airlines flight, and, of course, "Do Buy" at its massive duty-free malls. Just don't mind its impossible heat!

As bad as Dubai's heat is for tourists, it is another thing altogether for Dubai's expat population living their day-to-day lives. For one thing, death by heat stroke is depressingly common. There are no official figures on heat-stroke deaths, and the casualties are generally the poorest of the poor. Most are the foreign construction labourers who work outdoors in the intense heat. There is no escape for these people, even when they return to their labour camps in the evening, as their rooms may or may not even have a window air-conditioning unit. Most of these workers spend their weekends just sitting in Dubai's huge, glittering, air-conditioned shopping malls simply to get out of the heat.

Even for those who have access to air conditioning, whether in the form of central air or window units, they need to use it constantly and continuously for at least nine months of the year, and this can also have serious negative effects on the body and its health. Air conditioning cools the human body and provides relief from both heat and perspiration. In short, by preventing the body from being used to cooling itself naturally through sweating, when you do go outside, your body is ill-equipped to handle it. In addition, sweating is facilitated and controlled by the kidneys, and the constant use of air conditioning impairs the kidney's ability to do its job. This can damage it over time and lead to diseases such as high blood pressure, which is caused by a malfunctioning kidney.

These kinds of conditions are only made worse by the generally sedentary lifestyle in Dubai. It is difficult to go outside and stay active in the incredible heat. It is difficult to even do something as simple as take a brisk walk late at night without getting completely drenched in sweat.

Finally, the heavy use of air conditioning requires a great deal of electricity, which of course costs money. Historically, such utilities were heavily subsidised by the government for both locals and the expats. However, with the Gulf states reeling under the impact of low oil prices, they have eliminated subsidies for all utilities and are allowing the utility markets to correct themselves in line with the international prices of related markets. As a result, electricity and water prices have gone up for all residents of the UAE, whether they are citizens or foreigners.

There is also a slightly sinister side to the utility pricing, as well. For example, as of November 2016, locals in Abu Dhabi paid 5 fils per KwH of electricity, while expats paid 21 fils per KwH—four times what the locals paid. Under the new rules, the locals will pay 6.7 fils per KwH, and foreigners will pay 26.8 fils per KwH.

Similarly, as of November 2016, locals in Dubai paid Dhs 2.09 per cubic metre for water, while foreigners paid Dhs 5.95 per cubic metre. Under the new water rates, locals' water prices will not change, while foreigners will start paying Dhs 7.84 per cubic metre for water.

Since foreigners make up 90 percent of the UAE's total population, it doesn't take a rocket scientist to realize that the foreign population is subsidising the locals' water and other utility costs.[53]

---

53. You can read more about utility pricing in the UAE here: www. thenational.ae/uae/abu-dhabi-residents-face-utility-price-rises-1.205101.

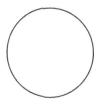

DUBAI AND RELIGION

Dubai is an international melting pot of cultures and people from all around the world, and one of the best things about it is that it is a relatively religiously tolerant place. The government of Dubai has given special permission for a Christian church and a Hindu temple, which doubles as a Sikh *gurudwara*, to be built within the city so that people of other religions can follow their own beliefs. These buildings are required to be fairly non-descript normal residential or commercial properties, so that anyone looking at them from the outside would not think they are places of worship.

Members of non-Muslim religions are also allowed to publicly gather at designated public places to celebrate their religious holidays. Before a major celebration, such as the Hindu festival of Durga Puja, the organizers have to seek permission from the Dubai municipality. However, the authorities are more interested in knowing how many people will be gathering than in what god they will be praying to. This is mostly due to a fear of public demonstrations sowing dissent and discord in the wake of the Arab Spring. As a result, a peaceful religious gathering is not considered a problem, and such permission is always granted. These privileges for other religious groups have been in place since the previous ruler, the late Sheikh Rashid, permitted non-Muslims to have their own places of worship.

That said, to our knowledge, there are no Jewish places of worship in Dubai at all. This is largely a political issue, rather than a religious one, though. Judaism is a religion associated with Israel, and all six Gulf countries are officially sworn enemies of Israel.

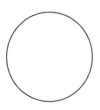

HOW TO BEAT THE DUBAI TRAP: A STRATEGY FOR MAXIMIZING YOUR STAY IN DUBAI AND BECOMING SUPER-RICH WITH YOUR DIGNITY INTACT

Now that you are thoroughly acquainted with the realities of life in Dubai, we would like to offer some final thoughts, tips, and suggestions for three different segments of the Dubai expatriate community: the employees of firms and companies who operate there, business professionals who own various businesses in Dubai, and investors. This section is especially relevant for the millions of people from around the globe who plan to make Dubai their temporary residence in the wake of Dubai's Expo2020 and /or trying to pursue a career/ employment/business there. Hopefully, these newcomers will benefit from this section and will not have to go through the painful learning curve that those who have been in Dubai for a while had to go through.

For readers interested in property investment in Dubai, whether it is for residential or commercial purposes, remember that buying property in Dubai does *not* give the property owner the indefinite right to reside in Dubai. Residence visas are granted for three years if the property is over a certain value, and the visa can be renewed after that if the owner is still in possession of the property, but that is it. Owning property does not grant any special rights in the country.

In addition, before purchasing any property in Dubai, be sure you address the following issues and consider the following questions:

1. Buying property is a long-term investment, and as such, rules and regulations handle inheritance issues. You not only need to research what these regulations are like now, but also consider what they might be like for foreigners in Dubai twenty or thirty years from now. Find out what will happen if the current property owner dies suddenly and how the family will inherit the property.

2. What is the real value of the property? Who performed the valuation? How does it compare to an equivalent property in a more culturally inclusive part of the world with a moderate climate, such as Spain, France, Portugal, Costa Rica, or Malaysia? Can the firm that

performed the valuation stand by their assessment in both the short- and long-term?

3. What is the purchase price of the property? At that price, could the purchaser have bought an equivalent property in another country with a more open attitude toward potential immigrants?

4. What is the UAE's long-term future as a country? How will issues like oil prices affect its economy? How will climate change affect its liveability? How will geo-political situations affect Dubai? Do the answers to these questions justify a long-term investment in property in that country?

5. What is the resell value of the property? What are the laws governing property sales? What happens if there is a need to make a quick or distressed sale? Is there a well-developed property marketplace where both buyers and sellers can get a fair deal? What happens if the property is bought with a mortgage, and the property owners cannot pay their mortgage? What would happen to the property if the owner was based in Dubai, lost his job, and had checks bounce? If the bank does not receive its mortgage payment on time, does the property owner go to jail?

6. Most properties in Dubai are new constructions. In such cases, does the property seller provide a guarantee on the quality of the construction? Dubai is essentially a desert; are properties built on sand or soil? What are the implications for the long-term value of the property

(i.e., its structural longevity and value)? Is there any chance that the value of the property will disappear in the quicksands of the desert? In addition, Dubai's skyscrapers have been catching fire a great deal in recent years, as have those in other fast-growing cities in the United Arab Emirates. In 2015, two high-rises, The Torch and the Regal Towers, both went up in flames. As the world was seeing out 2015 on New Year's Eve, another Dubai skyscraper caught fire right besides the world's tallest building, Burj Khalifa. The New Year's Eve fireworks display went ahead as planned anyway. In fact, there have been at least thirty major fires reported in Dubai and the northern emirates between 2012 and 2017, yet there seems to be relatively little interest in investigating the causes for these fires. Are they the result of criminal behaviour? Are they caused by using unsafe and highly flammable materials in the buildings' construction? Dubai's government does not seem interested in the answers.[54]

Strangely, nothing is ever said in the news about the residents of these buildings. Deaths are never reported, so what happened to the residents? What became of their belongings? Did the government re-house them? What happened to the advance rent residents had

---

54. You can read more about these fires here: https://uk.reuters.com/article/ uk-dubai-fire/blaze-sweeps-through-dubai-skyscraper-for-second-time- idUKKBN1AJ34I.

already paid for the year? This complete silence on the issue is Dubai's style of dealing with unfortunate events like these. The only thing reported about these fires after the fact is when the building's owners get an insurance settlement.

In contrast, consider what happened when a similar tragedy struck Grenfell Towers in London. The whole community was dumbfounded by the inferno and rallied around the people affected. From A-list celebrities to regular people, everyone came together to support the victims—an example of a social safety net that Dubai simply does not have.

7. Think about things like deed documents, land registry documents, and titles. What language are they written in? Where are they held? What are the courts of jurisdiction in the event of a dispute, which is very common in Dubai? Who are entitled to have property deeds in their own name and in which part of Dubai ?

8. If you are a property investor or speculator trying to make money by quickly flipping property, you will need to do even more research than those considering property as a long-term investment. When Dubai's property bubble burst in 2008, expat speculators and property flippers lost almost everything.

9. Ask yourself why you want to buy property in what is essentially an uninhabitable desert, where life can barely survive without modern technology, and where temperatures regularly hit 54 degrees centigrade (130

degrees Fahrenheit)—or higher—with 100 percent humidity. Consider that even within the local population, if they have any money at all, they head to cooler parts of the world starting in June and do not return to Dubai until mid-September. With that in mind, what is so appealing about purchasing property here?

Experts predict that most of the UAE will become completely uninhabitable by the turn of the current century due to global warming. Only the highly developed and extremely air-conditioned cities of Dubai and Abu Dhabi will be able to survive. In addition, ground water is rapidly running out, which could soon lead to water shortages.[55] Do you still want to make a long-term property investment in a country that will be almost entirely uninhabitable?[56]

Even the sea in the area has warmed thanks to global warming, and Western war ships are already finding it difficult to navigate such warm waters. Consider what kind of inheritance, if any, you would be passing on to your heirs.

If at all possible, before making a long-term property investment

---

55. To read more about this, see: www.dailymail.co.uk/wires/ap/
article-3331490/Parched-Emirates-relies-sea-groundwater-runs-out.html.
56. See this link for more details: www.msn.com/en-gb/news/world/
the-countries-that-will-be-so-hot-by-2100-humans-won't-be-able-to-go-
outside/ar-BBmtvd6?li=AA59G2&ocid=UP9.

in Dubai, ask a local who owns property in Dubai, if he had the money to buy more, where would he buy it? It's certainly understandable if he would want to buy a second home in a cooler climate, but would he consider buying an investment property in Dubai? Also, ask expats who have resided in the UAE for a long time if they would ever consider investing in property in the UAE and if they had bought one what do they think about that investment. Those on the ground in the country always know the realities of that property market best.[57]

Now that we have an understanding of the issues surrounding buying property in Dubai, let us turn to the strategies an "average" expat should follow in order to maximize their wealth and well-being in the UAE. This is intended as general guidance, as each person will face their own unique circumstances based on their country of origin, gender, ethnicity, career objectives, personal financial situation, etc. The following information has been collated after observing individuals from a wide cross-section of UAE expats over the years:

---

57. To get a better idea of what exactly is currently happening in the Dubai property market, see: www.albawaba.com/business/properties-prices-keep-falling-dubai-1154546, www.ft.com/content/cd4e49d8-6307-11e7-8814-0ac7eb84e5f1, and www.ft.com/content/f0b8a1d4-a9b1-11e7-ab66-21cc87a2edde.

1. Social and moral compliance with local official standards is of the utmost importance in Dubai. This can seem extreme, especially for those from the freer societies of the West. It is highly advisable for those who have issues with money management, drugs, or alcohol; those who plan to cohabit outside of marriage; or those who are in same-sex relationships to stay in their home countries. Sufficient examples of Dubai's attitude towards such "crimes" have been provided throughout, illustrating how the international community heading to Dubai for a holiday or long-term residence can be seriously affected by Dubai's ultra-conservative attitudes, despite its portraying itself as a super-sleek twenty-first century metropolis.

   In the course of an expat's life in the UAE, there can be no arguments in public, ever; no financial problems; no marital discord; no business failures; no falling out with business associates; and no expression of dissatisfaction over rude treatment by a local or a local government official. Your life must always seem like a deep-blue, sunshine-filled sky, without the slightest hint of a dark cloud anywhere. If there is ever even the slightest hint of something untoward, you need to be prepared for the possibility of jail time, because there is no social safety net for the foreigner.

   Even small vices, like gambling or watching porn on the internet, are punishable by imprisonment. Keep in mind that the internet is heavily monitored—especially in the wake of the Arab Spring—and any unsavory Google searches or complaints about the country on social media can lead to severe punishment.

In its own unique way, Dubai operates on something like a "Don't ask, don't tell" policy. No one will knock on your door and demand to know whether you are in a same-sex relationship or are cohabiting with a member of the opposite sex outside of legal matrimony. But if there is even a minor, completely unrelated event that involves you with the law—say, for example, an altercation with a taxi driver, a shouting match with your spouse in your own apartment, or the slightest dispute with a neighbour over parking—you could unexpectedly be subject to a criminal investigation for unlawful sexual behaviour. Of course, even a mild case of road rage or showing the other driver the middle finger can have disastrous consequences as well.

Most expats in same-sex or unmarried opposite-sex relationships who are caught in such situations usually simply claim that they are friends or relatives that are sharing the cost of the apartment. Many in unmarried heterosexual relationships claim that they are engaged or were married according to their own religious rites. All of these are perfectly acceptable, unless a local catches them engaged in a public display of affection. In such cases, the first question the police will ask is whether the couple has had sexual intercourse, and it is extremely important to be prepared for this, especially if you come from a country where such behaviour is considered private—which is basically the rest of the civilised world.

However, expats are most likely to get caught in these sorts of situations when there is a completely unrelated dispute about money, particularly when there is a powerful local who stands to benefit monetarily from the expat being traumatised by the Dubai legal nightmare.

In such cases, the local will use his *wasta* with the various law enforcement agencies in Dubai to demoralise and extort money from the expat. During such situations, it is important to first connect with your own personal network, which is usually your own national community. See if they can unearth another, more powerful local who is willing to use his *wasta* and talk to the police to provide a favourable and more realistic picture of the situation. If you can do this, more often than not, things can move very quickly in your favour, and the case can disappear as mysteriously as it first appeared. Suddenly, the police will start saying very positive things about you.

Remember that going to a lawyer under duress in Dubai can be a very expensive proposition and should be an act of last resort. Keep in mind that in all of this, we are talking about "Dubai Fake Crimes"—things that would not be a crime anywhere else in the world. For actual criminal allegations, like theft, murder, rape, etc., always contact your embassy first, if you are allowed to do so.

In general, keep your head down, stick to the straight and narrow, appear to be squeaky-clean, and keep extremely tight control over your money—far tighter than anywhere else in the world. If you can do this, hopefully you will return home wealthier than you left.

2. Before accepting an offer of employment in Dubai, negotiate very, very hard indeed. If you are offered a position that is lower than your current role, either in terms of your title or, most importantly, expected compensation, please, *please* resist the tax-free status, the allure of the endless sunshine, and the temptation of the luxurious Dubai lifestyle and give them a categorical NO in response, if your circumstances permit. Once you are in the UAE, you cannot renegotiate anything. You cannot ask for a raise or seek a promotion. There is a very, very high probability that you will remain in the exact same role and at the same salary forever, and once you have trained the locals on how to do your job, you will be expected to hand it over to them and leave the country, especially if you are working in a lucrative public sector position. Promotions and raises are for locals only. They might provide some temporary sweeteners to expats by giving them a small raise or elevating their job title slightly if they feel the locals have not yet mastered the role and need more time under the expat's tutelage. But once that has happened, off goes the

expat to wherever he came from.

3. If you are leaving a high-flying career in places like New York City, London, Berlin, Tokyo, or any other highly developed market to come to Dubai, I would strongly advise you to think twice unless you are being given a truly phenomenal tax-free employment and benefit package with which you can achieve a major life milestone. It should be so good, it should feel like winning the lottery. In addition, if there are personal issues, like a looming divorce or a serious need for a complete change of scenery, then Dubai might not be a bad place to temporarily relocate to get away from it for a while, after having carefully considered all issues.

Similarly, professionals in the developing world who are doing very well with global multinationals in their home countries should exercise maximum caution as well and should drive a very hard bargain when negotiating for a position in Dubai. You need to keep your own interests at the forefront of your mind and carefully consider your own long- and short-term career objectives.

Those who are nearing the autumn of their careers or unemployed or underemployed, no matter where they're from, should readily look at lucrative or even average offers in Dubai with a much more open mind. However, keep in mind that after a certain age, you will not be able to get an employment visa or renewal of an existing visa. After carefully making sure that all of your pensions, retirement accounts, and personal circumstances are in line, feel free to take your skills and experience to the Gulf and enjoy the sunshine there. If you can accumulate a nice additional nest egg over and above what you have already built up in the course of your career at home, it will be a great way to enhance the quality of your retirement.

Professionals who work in fast-changing niche fields like artificial intelligence, robotics, and related cutting-edge software and those who, in general, need to constantly upgrade their skills through continuous professional development and education should think carefully before making a move not only to Dubai but to anywhere in the Middle East.

Apart from trying to maximize your basic salary, try to lock down these issues in your negotiations as well:

a. Ask your prospective employers to provide accommodation comparable to what you are used to in your own country. This can often make or break a deal. Remember, the biggest source of inflation in the UAE is in the rental market. If you can get your accommodation paid for, it is an excellent hedge against inflation while also protecting your real income. However, this perk is nearly impossible to obtain these days and was much more common in the 1980s and 1990s. Those who cannot get their accommodation paid for should at least get their employers to provide them interest-free rent advances, which they can then pay back from their monthly salaries, and loans for soft and hard furnishings.

b. The next most unpredictable expense in the UAE is school fees for children. If your potential employers can guarantee that they will pay all school fees for your children, including annual tuition increases, it can be a great way to preserve your income.

c. Another major point you should address in your negotiations is the price of the air tickets for passage back home, depending on the nature of your employment contract. In senior roles, professionals should ask for first-class or at least business class annual return tickets for themselves and their eligible family members. There should be an option built into the contract for these to be paid in cash and not just in the form of the tickets themselves. That way, you can use the extra tax-free cash to travel freely. That flexibility will mean a better lifestyle and additional source of funds, for you and your family.

Of course, what you can get written into your employment contract very much depends on how valuable your skills are in Dubai at the time. For example, at the moment, specialists in block-chain technology or crypto-currency can and should start their negotiations by asking for a high basic income, plus paid accommodation. The best part about Dubai is that if you bargain hard enough, if they need your skills enough, and if you are at the top of your field, you will get it.

First, go to Dubai at your employer's invitation and

expense to see and experience the city in person. State your demands, and if they are not met, walk away if your circumstances permit and go back to your home country. Be patient. You will more than likely be pleasantly surprised to see them come back in three or four months, more than ready to meet all your demands.

In short, when negotiating an employment contract in Dubai, keep your eyes and ears open, ask a lot of questions about what could potentially burn a hole in your pocket once you're there, and negotiate very, *very* hard along those lines. It is okay to drive a hard bargain. Get the best possible "deal plus," as they say, before you take up your new post, as it is extremely difficult to re-negotiate anything once you have started. Securing all of these things in advance will help buffer you from inflation for at least a few years while also compensating you for the loss of skills, knowledge, and other professional growth that would have occurred had you continued at home.

You need to get these items written into the contract in advance. The cost of something over the entire period of the work contract should be the negotiating point, not the cost at the moment for one month or one year. Other things to consider negotiating for are health insurance/ health care and an annual bonus. Many companies pay all employees an annual bonus of around 20 percent of the gross annual salary.

4. Western expats and expats from fast-developing

nations should run a careful cost/benefit analysis before they even begin negotiations with a potential Gulf employer. They must take into consideration things like 1) the potential loss of career prospects, 2) stunted professional development and loss of trade skills, 3) the potential loss of their state and private pensions through loss of pension credits due to non-residential status , and 4) potential lost investment opportunities, such as acquisition of second or third properties, in their home country. This list is just a small sample of the factors to consider and bring to the negotiation table when finalizing relocation terms.[58]

As a ballpark figure, the minimum salary a Western expat should accept is twice the gross (not net) annual income, before taxation, that he is getting back home or that his particular job or skill set can attract in the West. There will be no salary increases once you are in Dubai unless you change jobs, which is never a smooth or easy process. The high inflation rate in Dubai will very quickly erode all chances of saving money.

Of course, this might be a different story if you are an employee of a large multinational company and are simply making an internal transfer with a comprehensive relocation package in place. In such

---

58. You can read more about Dubai's cost of living here: www.thenational. ae/business/travel-and-tourism/dubai-no-2-most-expensive-city-to-stay-in-report-says-1.605141.

cases, a couple of years in the UAE is not a problem, so long as there is a provision to be transferred back out at your previous or more senior level after a specified term. Also, keep in mind that professional experience in the UAE is not exactly highly sought internationally, due to the nature of the UAE's economy. With no taxes, no VAT[59], no clear transparent and constantly shifting regulations/standards, and hardly any complexity in the economy, most professionals lose their edge. For nearly all professions, professional decadence sets in after a few years in Dubai. It is all about money there, and working in Dubai does not prepare you for anything else.

Thus, from a career perspective, an expat's best strategy is to get a posting in the UAE for a few years, build up a tax-free nest egg to pay off your mortgage or student loans and build up a rainy day fund, and then persuade your parent company to provide a fresh international posting or send you back to your home country in a more senior role. If you happen to love the UAE lifestyle, then, by all means, try and continue on there as long as you like, so long as your employer can keep you there or you can use your local "Gulf experience," as it is called, to get another job in the Gulf.

---

59. Though this changed in 2018, when the UAE started imposing a 5 percent VAT on goods and services. You can read more about it here: www.thenational.ae/uae/vat-in-uae-residents-say-tax-on-water-and-electricity-will-add-to-rising-utility-bills-1.674562).

That said, it might make sense to leave the UAE after a while—say five years from a financial security point of view—if your personal situation permits. According to UAE labour law, all firms are required to pay a gratuity to all expat staff when they leave. This is equivalent to twenty days' salary per year for the first three years with the firm and thirty days' salary after three years of service. So if a person is working for a company in the UAE for ten years, that gratuity could build up to be a nice tax-free nest egg. If, for some reason, the firm goes bust before the employee leaves—as can happen in the UAE, or anywhere else in the world, even with large multinational companies—the expat will simply have to write off that money. Thus, it makes sense to grab these funds by leaving the job before the firm sinks and get it out of the UAE to a safer place. Then, you can return to the UAE with another fresh employment contract and possibly higher pay. All expats should always be actively considering a change of employment if they are looking for some form of progression in their earnings or status, especially if they are working in Dubai's/the UAE's public sector.

If you are not keen to return to your homeland, it is essential that you begin the process of looking for a permanent residence in countries that allow planned migration, like Canada, Australia, and New Zealand, as soon as possible. Since these immigration applications are age-sensitive, they should be done within a few years of arriving in Dubai. In general, immigration to these countries should be done by age thirty-five and definitely before forty. Otherwise, you might be seen as a drain on the health and social security systems of your targeted countries. Being in the UAE, an application has a higher chance of acceptance than if the person applies from their home country because of the UAE's perceived affluence. Once your immigration application has been approved, travel to your new homeland and get permanent rights of residence and a new passport. Once the residency formalities are complete, you can return to the Gulf and resume working there. Just remember the tax implications of such a move. For example, Canadians, we understand, are taxed on their worldwide income, not just on what is earned in Canada. If this planned migration is executed properly at a relatively young age, it can be a successful way of increasing your and your family's overall well-being and net worth and of creating a proper international lifestyle.

Also, keep in mind that job-hopping in Dubai is easier said than done. Everything depends on the visa regime, which can be manipulated by the whims and fancies of your current employer, who controls your visa. If you resign for another position, your employer must cancel your residency visa before your new employer can offer you a new one. However, you have no way of knowing what kind of cancellation stamp has been used on your passport. Thus, you could face the situation of coming back into the UAE and discovering that your previous employer has banned you from employment in the UAE for some unknown reason. Thus, use maximum caution during and after the visa cancellation process and transfer from one employer to another. Labour laws are extremely volatile.

5. Expats from India, Bangladesh, Pakistan, the Philipines, Sri Lanka and other developing nations should negotiate for at least the same salary in UAE currency they are grossing in their home countries. So, for example, a person getting a salary of Rupees 50,000 per month in India should ask for at least Dirhams 50,000 per month in Dubai.

6. People from developing nations should try to save at least half of their monthly salary in Dubai. Given the UAE's steep inflation, your savings potential—often the only reason to move to Dubai—will be further eroded every year. It is best to save as much as possible as soon as possible. This is especially true given that, over time, expats in Dubai move away from the level of consumption they were used to back home—which is nearly always less—and begin to spend at the local level of consumption, with at times catastrophic results.

7. It is best to open a non-resident account with the UAE branch of a bank headquartered in your home country. For example, for Indians, this could be Canara Bank or the State Bank of India. These institutions operate with different partners and brand names in the UAE.

Alternatively, bank with international banks, like Citi Corp, HSBC, or Standard Chartered Bank and send money back home from the very first payday. Do not keep money or assets in the UAE, other than an emergency fund equivalent to three months' gross expenses. Of course, this is all subject to one's individual circumstances. You should seek out credible professional financial planning advice at the earliest opportunity for everything mentioned in this book.

Western expats used to regulated, independent financial advisors should be warned that financial advisors of all shapes and sizes take advantage of the UAE's lax, constantly shifting rules and opaque regulations. Expats cannot expect much from a regulatory body in the event of unsuitable financial advice from unlicensed advisors, and in general, it is very difficult to decipher who is licensed and who is not. It might be better to go to brands like HSBC, Barclay's, or BNP Paribas, which have a global reputation to defend in the event a formal complaint is lodged and the local press becomes involved.[60]

---

60. The UAE insurance industry is currently facing a major shake-up due to an alarming number of complaints. Many expats were burned when they bought long-term investment products and the advisor's commission severely reduced their returns. In addition, their exit clauses barred them from cashing out when they realized fly-by-night operators had sold them unsuitable products. You can read more here: www.thenational.ae/business/uae-insurance-industry-faces-shakeup-after-alarming-amount-of-complaints-1.216820.

8. During your initial years in Dubai, keep your spending at a minimum—especially for those coming from developing nations—until you have built up a sizeable financial buffer back home. Keep all forms of conspicuous consumption aimed at copying the UAE locals' lifestyle—such as fancy watches, jewelry, glasses, and cars—on hold for at least three or four years until you have built up a solid savings nest-egg. If you like the job and like staying in the UAE, just keep your head down and take the approach of "see no evil, hear no evil, speak no evil." Don't make waves, and just keep making money, sending it back home on your payday, and hang around as long as you can or until you have attained your personal financial goals.

9. Resist the temptation to borrow money through credit cards and personal loans, as nearly unregulated, greedy multinational banks inundate expats with tempting loan offers. If you are very good with your finances and can manage your money extremely well, you can take up these loan offers and build assets back home. But if there is anything short of complete financial self-discipline and self-control, or if you use these borrowed funds for Dubai-style conspicuous consumption, this temptation and the slightest loss of focus could land even the most savvy of borrowers in jail.

Also, keep in mind that the banks' computer systems are directly connected to the Dubai Police, Immigration, and Labour Departments' computer systems. If you lose your job and, consequently, your residence visa is cancelled, the banks are immediately notified of this fact. They can and will impose a travel ban on you if there is even a very small outstanding financial liability.

10. Obtain a UAE driver's license as soon as possible. This is much easier for expats from the thirty-six nations whose licenses can be directly exchanged for a UAE license. With a driver's license, families can move further away from Dubai's increasingly high rents.

One of the best things about Dubai is its entrepreneurial energy, which generates a feeling that there is plenty of money to be made everywhere and from anything. Everyone says that anything can be done. It is almost infectious.

"Can we make this deal worth $60 million?"

"Of course. *Mafi Mushkil*, my friend."

"Can we get this $100 million project going?"

"No problem. *Mafi Mushkil*. Consider it done."

"Can we get this contract signed?"

Of course, when talk turns to written contracts, there is always a short hesitation. Then, "My brother, you are my friend. I trust you. My word is my bond. Trust me…" this is where the speaker's right hand goes up and touches the heart. "There is no need for a contract. Let's make millions first…"

Throughout the UAE and in Dubai's glittering hotel lobbies and restaurants, this is the normal way business is done. It is contagious and intoxicating, and unsuspecting individuals can really be suckered in. When you hear so many "Yes"s, even the most skeptical start to believe in miracles.

For example, two world-class boxers were recently offered a $40 million, once-in-a-lifetime deal to hold a prizefight in Dubai. They saw petrodollar signs, and without a contract in hand, they threw caution to the wind, quickly made plans, and rushed off to Dubai to pose for the cameras of both the international conventional media and the new social media, announcing their fight to the whole world. A few days later, the so-called deal unraveled. One can only imagine how much these boxers' PR teams had already shelled out for hotels and transportation expenses for their entourages.

Similarly, another well-known boxer recently went to Dubai and was supremely impressed by its glamorous buildings and glittering hotels. Convinced that there was money to be made there and lulled by the easy assurances of local businessmen, he thoughtlessly signed off on a seven-digit personal check toward a business venture in Dubai. When the check bounced, he was locked up in Bur Dubai's police station for a few days. Of course, having a great deal of money, international recognition, and *wasta*, his stay behind the bars did not last long.

Similarly, a tennis legend went bankrupt when a residential construction project in Dubai that he lent his name—and his money—to went bust. It took out quite a large chunk of his hard-earned estate.

It is very true that the UAE and Dubai offer a gateway to some of the biggest markets in the world. Its apparent lack of red tape, free wheeler-dealer economy, zero restrictions on foreign exchange remittances, zero personal taxes(till date), and nearly zero crime make it a very attractive base from which to operate. But the reality may be slightly different.

Here are some tips for legitimate businesses trying to expand their operations in that part of the world:

1. When setting up a business in the UAE, be very careful about getting into a sponsorship deal with a private local. This can be a very risky proposition, similar to an arranged marriage, and the only way it will truly work out to your benefit is through sheer luck. This is not to demean locals in general, and many businesses have enjoyed sound, long-term relationships with their local sponsors. But there are also plenty who don't. Once the local sponsor sees the business flourishing, it is not uncommon for natural human greed to kick in, and suddenly, there is an ongoing, steady increase in demands for sponsorship money. Since everything is in the hands of the local sponsor—from visas to bank accounts—it can be extremely difficult to operate, and every new demand for money will feel like systematic blackmail, which, in reality, is what it is.

2. A good course of action is to find a reasonably priced Free-Trade Zone. The one nearest Dubai, the Jebel Ali Free-Trade Zone, is the most established and also the most expensive. Free-Trade Zones are run by the regional governments, and they can issue visas for a fixed annual fee and rent out virtual offices, which will provide a post office box. This process is supposed to take out the personal-greed factor associated with

some local sponsors. In the initial stages of setting up a business in the UAE, it is best to hunt for Free-Trade Zones in the neighboring northern emirates, like Fujairah, Ras al-Khaimah, and Ajman. Sharjah also has a Free-Trade Zone, but it is socially very strict and more along the lines of Saudi Arabia than Dubai, which in a way is not a bad thing, as it sets realistic expectations. Dubai's shiny outward veneer promises Las Vegas and delivers a prehistoric monster.[61]

3. The best business model for those in the initial stages of operating in Dubai is the "suitcase banking" model promoted by Pakistani bank BCCI in the 1980s. They replicated this model in India, where they were granted a license to open a branch in Mumbai. From there, their executives flew to Calcutta or Delhi with their briefcases each morning do business in those cities and then returned to Mumbai by the evening flight. It was a very successful business model until the bank was shut down due to serious allegations of laundering drug money.

The "suitcase banking" model is ideal for establishing a business in Dubai. Start by purchasing a Transit Visa, which are valid for up to fourteen days. Then follow this

---

61. As an example, here are some details about the Ras al Khaimah Free-Trade Zone. This is not intended as a recommendation, just as supplying information that businesses can take into account when they are conducting further market research: www.rakez.com/Promotions/Special-Offer-FB/Li-Dis-Rem.

up by surveying and assessing what appears to be—on the surface—a highly dynamic and red-tape-free market with huge liquidity. It does not matter where the person tasked with conducting this survey of the Dubai market is based—it could be London, New York, Mumbai, Rio, Nairobi, etc. They just need to be able to move in and out of the country as they assess the market's suitability and then build a proper rationale for doing business in Dubai.

Once that initial survey can provide a fair idea of what needs to be done to establish a business in Dubai, a three-month Visit Visa can be purchased and used to drum up business for the principal entity, which is still based outside of the UAE. After spending at least six-to-nine months on the ground, which amounts to two or three Visits Visas, you will be in a good position to decide whether to set up an operation in Dubai/the UAE.

4. Every legitimate business going into Dubai must get its license word-perfect. Nothing should get lost in translation, especially if it is an even slightly complex type of business. Do not listen to your local sponsor, even if they assure you with things like, "You are my brother. Believe me, this is the correct license. I will never let you down." Pay the extra few hundred Dirhams for a legal or judicial translation from Arabic to English of the exact licensing terms that are being issued.

The exact wording of a trading license might seem

like a frivolous issue in the heady excitement of setting up a business in one of the most glamorous cities in the world, but when the dust settles and the cold realities of doing business in Dubai creep in, those few hundred Dirhams for a legal translation may turn out to be the wisest you ever spent in Dubai. If there is ever the need to take a business associate to court or deal with a dispute with an employee, having a word-perfect trading license will help immeasurably. It can help you or your business avoid a high fine and even keep you out of jail. Dubai government officials often raid offices based on malicious complaints and impose hefty fines on foreign businesses without properly investigating or understanding the business model. Needless to repeat, there is no right of appeal for such unfair victimisations.

5. Make sure that all business deals are written in airtight contracts and preferably backed up by a post-dated check. This is essential if you want to get paid. When a deal is being discussed in Dubai, a lot of it is verbal. You will frequently hear assurances like, "You are my brother. Can't you not trust me?" "My word is my bond. Ask anyone in Dubai," "I am swearing by touching this drinking water, the moment you deliver, I will pay your fees," "I swear on my children's health that I have never let down anyone with money."

But once the goods or services are delivered, there is often a very long silence. It is not uncommon for clients to not pick up the phone or answer emails if there is a big payment due. If work is done on the basis of a verbal commitment, there is often no intention of ever paying. With nothing in writing, you cannot lodge a complaint with the authorities. In short, it is a good old-fashioned con job. In fact, payment defaults are one of the biggest problems in doing business in the UAE, for companies both big and small. Every year thousands of small and medium sized businesses owned by expats meet their untimely demise when a bigger local firm goes bankrupt or refuses to honour its payment commitments.

For example, the global UK-based conglomerate Carillion went bankrupt in February 2018 with losses of nearly a thousand jobs. Because it was such a major financial debacle, Carillion's senior management was quizzed by the UK's Parliament about what had happened. The firm's management claimed that one of the reasons for the firm's collapse was the non-payment of £200 million from a Qatar firm after a project was completed—of course, the Qatar firm denies this.[62]

This is how business is done all throughout the Gulf countries. Firms purchasing the goods or services can and do refuse to make promised payments, often for frivolous and, at times, no reason, after work has been completed or goods supplied. This can have a devastating impact on the supplier firm that carried

---

62. You can read the full story here: https://qatarileaks.com/en/leak/carillion-gave-uk-government-early-warning-of-qatar-payment-problems.

out the activities they were contracted for. The attitude could best described as one of, "Do what you can, but we will not pay." If it's not written on paper, it's a good as gone. Even if it is written on paper it is as good as gone if there is no supporting check or a banking instrument like letter of credit or letter of guarantee.

One of the best ways to avoid this is to get a post-dated check to cover the cost of the invoice or the goods to be supplied in advance. Then, if the firm refuses payment for some reason, it will be much more difficult for them. If they do not have the funds, they will be the ones in trouble for writing a check that bounces. Also, if millions of dollars-worth of goods are changing hands, it is imperative to get a letter of credit from them, signed off by a respectable international or Dubai government bank as a minimum form of security. International businesses based outside the UAE should follow this policy fervently. No goods or services, especially high-value ones, should be shipped into the UAE without appropriately confirmed and accepted payment instruments issued by top banks in the UAE, namely NBD Emirates or NBAD—the National Bank of Dubai and the National Bank of Abu Dhabi, respectively— or international banks like HSBC, Citi, and Standard Chartered etc.

6. Be careful when talking about business matters. There are thousands of mini-mafias operating in Dubai, comprised of both locals and expats of all nationalities,

and the police could not care less, so long as they do not spill any blood. Many of these mafia agents act as "brokers," "commission agents," "consultants," and "self-employed workers." They will often engage you in some sort of business conversation, start making verbal assurances of what they can do for you or your business, and then suddenly appear in your office and demand money for work they have never done. This will then be followed by threats and sabotage, like making false complaints to the police, if they are not paid. This is essentially crude blackmail, and this kind of extortion affects small enterprises most. Expats are generally too scared to go to the police, because it may end up with a case being lodged against them. If you are in a stable position with a respectable employer in Dubai, exercise maximum caution before making a move into Dubai's murky business world.

7. Even after a company has decided to establish an operational base in Dubai or the UAE, it should be run like a very tight ship. To be fair to Dubai, this should be the case for all businesses all over the world; however, in Dubai, this should be doubly true. Head counts should be kept to bare minimum due to very opaque labour laws, which can also turn an enterprise's orderly wind-down into a nightmare. Any employee can start a false and vexatious litigation with the help of a local and demand a payment from his employer to put an end to it—a kind of extortion we've previously discussed. If

backed by a powerful local or a lawyer, the case will more than likely go to court. Whether or not the firm wins, valuable time and resources will have to be diverted to defend a frivolous claim.

8. Additionally, a word of caution about copyright and intellectual property rights. It is very difficult to protect trade secrets in Dubai. Whether it is a supplier source, a special formula, a potential patent, or an effective business practice, it is nearly impossible for a business to maintain its unique selling proposition and progress. This is partially due to the entrepreneurial spirit of Dubai. Every employee believes they have the right to their employer's trade secrets and client base, and all they have to do to make some extra money on the side is to take a small office of their own and get to work with what would be considered proprietary information in other countries. There is no law in place to stop this kind of behaviour. After all, Dubai is all about money, free trade, and free enterprise.

For example, in a personal interview, John D'Souza told me how he had set up a very successful consultancy business, the first of its kind in Dubai. His banker had full access to his confidential business secrets, and he contacted one of John's clients who was refusing to make a payment. Together, they used Dubai's shady police world to lodge a series of malicious complaints against John. His business had to shut down, and the banker went on to use John's confidential business information

LOOKING TO THE FUTURE

Dubai's future is not an assured one. In fact, the climate itself is a threat to the very existence of Dubai in the long-term and to doing business there in the short-term. Popular folklore holds that Hitler lost the Second World War because of Russia's "General Winter." When the harsh Russian winter set in, even the well-equipped German soldiers were no match for the Russian soldiers, who had far less firepower than their German counterparts. The same thing happened to Napoleon's French troops when they tried to invade Russia. History has taught us not to mess around with nature, yet entrepreneurs head to Dubai in hordes and even purchase property there as an investment for the future, even though, by the turn of this century, most of the area will be completely uninhabitable due to global warming. An already very hot region, it will be pounded even further by global climatic changes that will only raise the temperature

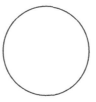

further. It is not going to be a pleasant experience for anyone. In time, Dubai's "General Summer" could very well beat us all, especially "property flippers." Businesses, professionals, and long-term investors need to take this climatic risk into serious consideration before setting up shop in Dubai.

Another major threat to the region comes from the very source of its wealth: oil. In the past, the Saudi Arabian-led coalition of the six Gulf AGCC nations—Saudi Arabia, Kuwait, the UAE, Qatar, Bahrain, and Oman—could control oil prices and hold the rest of the world to ransom. However, the emergence of the US's horizontal shale-oil fracking technology, also known as tight-oil exploration technology, has revolutionized the oil industry in the US and has been a complete game-changer and disruptor for global oil markets. Thanks to this new technology, the US could very well become self-sufficient in their oil needs, and even potentially the largest oil producer in the world, producing as much as ten million barrels or more per day. Considering that the US is currently the biggest consumer of Middle Eastern oil, this is not good news for the region.

Looking to the future, Saudi Arabia and its Gulf allies' ability to control oil prices by switching the oil tap on and off may soon be a thing of the past. With fracking technology in the mix, there will soon be five major players in the fossil-fuel market: Saudi Arabia and its brethren in the Gulf, the core of the OPEC cartel; the United States; Russia; the massive, multi-billion-dollar hedge funds that take both long- and short-term positions in oil futures; and finally, the producers of the humble lithium batteries that power Elon Musk's electric-car revolution.

In addition, as the other major oil buyers, like India, China, and EU, are seeing how the US shale-oil industry is shaking things up, they are forming their own buyers' clubs.

As global journalist Tim Worstall noted in *Forbes*, the economic purpose of running an oil cartel (or any cartel, for that matter) is to control prices. In the past, whenever there was a global oversupply of fossil fuel, OPEC would shut off production. With diminished supply, oil prices would go up. That time is now well and truly over, as OPEC does not control enough of the oil market anymore. As Worstall explains, economic monopolies or cartels are always brought down by changing technology. In short, the new fracking technology has challenged OPEC's power. The revolution of electric cars will likely drive the final nail into OPEC's coffin. After decades of dominating the global energy market, OPEC now stands on the edge of an abyss.

Improvements in fracking technology have improved productivity and made shale oil profitable even as global oil prices have dropped; in addition, there is the powerful "Seven and Seven Cocktail" Worstall describes. This refers to the fact that, using fracking technology, it takes seven months to get oil out of a new oil field, whereas using conventional technology, which is what most of OPEC relies on, it takes seven years.

In July 2014, the price of oil was around US$120 per barrel. In early 2018, it was in the mid-to-upper US$60s, though the OPEC cartel has desperately been trying to manipulate the prices, and as of June 2018, it is up to the upper US$70s per barrel. Still, assuming that oil has gone down an average of about

US$50 per barrel over the last four years, some basic math will show how this is going to pan out for the region as a whole.

The Gulf countries produce an average of twenty million barrels of oil per day. Roughly translated, oil standing at US$50 per barrel in 2017 against a price of at least US$100 per barrel in 2014 means that these six countries have hemorrhaged a total revenue of US$50 X 20 million per day, i.e., US$1 billion per day. With that kind of loss, a revenue stream of US$1 trillion has been wiped from the regional coffers in the last three years. This is not a small change, even by the wealth standards of Riyadh, Abu Dhabi, Kuwait City, and Doha, all put together.

Initially, these countries tried to keep US shale oil out of the game by swamping the market. That did not subdue US oil production though, and oil prices went down to US$26 per barrel. When that did not work, OPEC joined forces with Russia to ration global oil production so that oil prices went up again. In response, the US simply ramped up its own oil production. As of early 2018, it is producing just over 10 million barrels per day—the highest US oil production in the last forty years. Also, because OPEC reduced their own oil production, the US stepped in and captured the markets they had abandoned. For the first time in forty years, the US is exporting oil. It is a classic Catch-22 situation for OPEC: if they increase oil production, oil prices will go down; if they decrease oil production, their global market share will get gobbled up by the US.

Furthermore, the fact that fossil fuels may become irrelevant as a form of energy by the turn of this century is not good news for the leadership of this region. Could this affect the standard

246

of living for their citizens? If shale oil and fracking technology continue to keep oil prices down, can this region continue to experience the prosperity of the past few decades in the future? Ironically, the biggest threat to Dubai is Saudi Arabia. Dubai markets itself as a major tourist destination and international airline hub, and Saudi Arabia is starting to open up its economy to tourism to combat the loss of oil revenue. The Saudis are building better and classier hotels, and they already have quite a few historical sites to offer tourists. They are also building the tallest building in the world to usurp Dubai's Burj Khalifa's status of world's tallest building. Of course, unlike Dubai, they still will not offer alcohol to tourists, but that will actually work in their favour, as more conservative tourists do not like Dubai's half-baked, neither-here-nor-there attitude. Just before this book went into its final edit, Saudi Arabia re-opened its first cinema after thirty-five years and allowed women to drive for the first time in its history. All of this is the initiative of the young Sheikh Mohammed of Saudi, a thirty-year-old who has taken the personal mandate to take his country into the new millennium.

For its part, Dubai and its leadership team are already bracing for a life without high oil prices. Besides, Dubai never had much oil wealth, so it is actually less of an issue for this emirate than for many other parts of the region. Plus, Sheikh Mohamed and his team are already looking forward to a new technological boom to help drive their city and hoping that Dubai becomes the Silicon Valley of the Desert.

In 2016, Sheikh Mohamed's team announced that drones

would be ferrying individual passengers across Dubai by
July 2017 to reduce traffic congestion. The fact that Dubai
International Airport had already been shut down several times
by drone incursions did not matter, so long as this new toy could
be made available and shown off to the whole world, further
pushing Dubai's high-tech brand. Of course, like so many such
plans, this has not come to fruition.

When it comes to dreams of a technocratic future, Dubai is
always punching above its weight. One extreme example of this
is Sheikh Mohamed's recent announcement of his nation's plans
for a trip to Mars and potential colonization of the red planet.
It is claimed that one of the main reasons for this is to help ease
youth unemployment in the Middle East, an ongoing problem
that contributed, in part, to the Arab Spring uprisings.

Like all great Dubai dreams and plans, this Mars project
raises many questions:

1. If Mars becomes a UAE/Dubai colony, what types of
    visas would we need to get to Mars?
2. Who will actually do the work there? Poor Indians,
    Pakistanis, Bangladeshis,Filipinos and Sri Lankans?
    Poor (*miskin*) Martians?
3. Can Mercedes and Porsche adapt their cars for the
    Martian roads? After all, Dubai locals love their cars.
4. Who will be the real locals in Mars—the current UAE
    'asli' or Mars's original inhabitants?

Of course, some of these questions are tongue-in-cheek, but
they reflect the very serious social, economic, and political

248

issues that drive Dubai today.

Still, we're sure that Dubai's government will get everything sorted out. After all, everything is achievable in Dubai—from the tallest building in the world, to a year-round ice-skating rink in a desert. Nothing is ever a problem and everything is always possible in Dubai. At least, that's what they want you to believe. Why should Mars be any different? Perhaps one day, we will all be doing business in Dubai's glittering Martian spaceport and hotels, as trillions of Martian-dollars dance before our eyes and we imagine all of the endless possibilities in this new, entrepreneur-driven desert. After all, when it comes to Dubai and making money, the more things change, the more they stay the same.

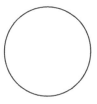

ABOUT THE AUTHOR

Originally from India, Sujit Shome is a graduate in Economics from Presidency College, Calcutta and went on to complete his MBA from FMS, Delhi. Sujit continued his professional development in London and successfully completed his Level 4 Diploma in Regulated Financial Planning from CII. He also holds professional certifications in Securities & Derivatives from CISI and Mortgage Advice (CeMAP & CERER) from IFS. Over the course of his career, Sujit has engaged with multiple business models, primarily in finance and banking and spent over a decade working in Dubai. It's this latter experience that he is keen to share with his readers, with a hope that it can make an informed difference to their lives in that city.

Sujit currently lives and works in London.

Dubai: An Insider's Guide is his first book.

SUJIT SHOME

Don't forget, you can get in touch with Sujit via social media:

On Instagram:
www.instagram.com/sujitshomeauthor

On Twitter:
www.twitter.com/sujit40s

He looks forward to hearing from you!